MW00834390

AN ANTHOLOGY OF ELIZABETHAN POETRY

AN ANTHOLOGY OF ELIZABETHAN POETRY

Edited by

SUKANTA CHAUDHURI

DELHI
OXFORD UNIVERSITY PRESS
BOMBAY CALCUTTA MADRAS
1992

Oxford University Press, Walton Street, Oxford OX2 6DP

New York Toronto
Delhi Bombay Calcutta Madras Karachi
Kuala Lumpur Singapore Hong Kong Tokyo
Nairobi Dar es Salaam
Melbourne Auckland
and associates in
Berlin Ibadan

Computerset by Rastrixi, New Delhi 110030
Printed in India at Rekha Printers Pvt. Ltd., New Delhi 110020
and published by S.K. Mookerjee, Oxford University Press
YMCA Library Building, Jai Singh Road, New Delhi 110001

Contents

The Elizabethan Sonnet

Sir Philip Sidney: *Astrophil and Stella*

Edmund Spenser: *Amoretti*

Samuel Daniel: *Delia*

Michael Drayton: *Idea*

William Shakespeare: *Sonnets*

THE EPYLLION

Preface

This collection has been compiled with the college or university student in mind. But I hope it will appeal to a wider readership, as handy anthologies of Elizabethan poetry are not as common as one might wish.

'Elizabethan' is a flexible term: this book contains pieces published as late as 1630. As Metaphysical poetry is being reserved for a separate volume, I have had space for a wide choice of other authors and poetic types: fair amounts of Spenser and Drayton, *The Mirror for Magistrates*, pastoral and epyllion, as well as the customary sonnets and lyrics.

There are few conventions to explain. The letter *n* after a line reference indicates the note on that line. References in bold Arabic numerals are to the pieces as numbered in this book.

The book was begun while I was Visiting Professor at Delhi University. I must thank the English Department and the University Library there for their hospitality. I completed the work at Presidency College, Calcutta. My thanks, as always, to its library staff, and more improbably to its Physics and Zoology Departments for admitting the Elizabethan virus to their computers.

SUKANTA CHAUDHURI

Introduction

I: TRADITIONS AND INFLUENCES

The age of 'Elizabethan' poetry does not coincide with the reign of Queen Elizabeth I from 1558 to 1603. The earliest notable poetry of this type was produced by Wyatt and Surrey in the days of Henry VIII. The movement became forceful only in the latter part of Elizabeth's reign, and continued in the time of James I (*r.* 1603–25) and Charles I (*r.* 1625–42), though certain new tendencies gradually transformed its course.

If we still call this body of poetry Elizabethan, it is partly from habit; but the habit grew in the first place because Elizabeth's reign seems best to exemplify the social and cultural forces that created this poetry.

Medieval English poetry reached its greatest height in the late fourteenth century. This was the age of Chaucer, Gower and Langland, of *Pearl* and *Sir Gawain and the Green Knight*, and of a rich body of romance, lyric poetry and religious drama. These lines of writing continued in the fifteenth century, but in subdued form. The English Chaucerians, such as Thomas Hoccleve (1369?–1426), John Lydgate (*c.* 1370– *c.* 1450) and Stephen Hawes (1475–1523), largely rework the old themes and motifs, seldom in a truly vigorous or original way. On the whole, the Scottish Chaucerians provide a livelier output: King James I of Scotland (1394–1437), Robert Henryson (*c.* 1420–*c.* 1490), William Dunbar (*c.* 1460–*c.* 1520), Gavin Douglas (*c.* 1475–1522), Sir David Lyndsay (*c.* 1485–1555). (It must be remembered that at this time Scotland was a separate sovereign state.) But it remains true that English (and Scottish) poetry could not acquire any significant new direction in the fifteenth or early sixteenth century.

Much of the problem lay in the fact that the English language had markedly changed its nature between the fourteenth and sixteenth centuries—or, to put it more accurately, changes which had been taking place over many centuries had finally reached a watershed. The grammatical structure of Old English, which had been disintegrating right through the Middle English period, now lost its last vestiges of inflectional endings (which accounted for the puzzling *e*'s at the end of many words in Chaucer and other Middle English writers). Still more fundamentally, there was a major vowel shift in the fifteenth and early sixteenth centuries (continuing, indeed, into the early seventeenth century) whereby nearly all the long vowels in English came to be pronounced in new ways.

All this threw the phonetic (and hence metrical) system of the language out of gear. There was also the continuing problem of a multiplicity of dialects—only the first uncertain steps had been taken towards a 'standard' or 'King's' English—and the printing press had heightened the discrepancy between sound and spelling. Further, the Renaissance saw a huge influx of new words and affixes that the poets had to assimilate. In a word, the resources of the language as a whole were being powerfully enlarged even as the old resources lost their efficacy and the old linguistic order was cast into confusion. English Renaissance poetry was born out of this state of creative flux. The relatively barren years of the early and mid-sixteenth century were carrying out a crucial process of assimilation, whose results emerged triumphantly in the last two decades.

The impetus to develop these new resources came from tantalizing poetic models appearing on the Continent in Latin, Italian, French and Spanish. It is risky to label such models 'classical' or 'Renaissance', for they had complex origins, often in the Middle Ages. It seems better to call them, vaguely but safely, the 'new poetry'. I shall treat later of some important genres, themes and conventions of this poetry. Let us first look at the way it was transmitted and circulated.

Latin was the chief language of intellectual activity in Renaissance Europe. It had been so in the Middle Ages as well; but while medieval Latin was variable and often 'impure', the Renaissance sought to restore classical literary Latin. Again, the Middle Ages had known the important classical Latin poets, especially Virgil and Ovid, but read them in the light of medieval Christianity. The Renaissance attempted to revive their genuine spirit. It also made revolutionary discoveries of new poets and texts, as well as better texts of the poets already known. Moreover, it asserted the importance of Greek poetry as the origin and governing force of the better-known and more widely-circulated Latin works.

This deeper understanding was important in itself; more so its effects on the new poetry being produced. First of all, there was a substantial line of new Latin (Neo-Latin) poetry right through the Renaissance which, at its finest, achieved remarkable power and originality.[1]

More importantly, Neo-Latin poetry acted as a controlling and vitalizing force behind poetry in the vernaculars. The crucial power of Renaissance classicism lay in that it inseminated fresh work in the new languages of modern Europe—a creative rather than restrictive or conservative force. Hence we find a range of extraordinarily fruitful compounds between new classical models and those descended in a direct line from the Middle Ages (though the latter may also go back to classical times). The vernaculars in which these developments took place earlier—Italian above all—could then act as independent influences on those (like English) that developed later, interacting with the 'medieval' elements special to the latter. Thus the corpus of European Renaissance poetry constitutes an awesome network of interacting lines and influences: classical, medieval, Neo-Latin and new vernacular, their numerous elements operating in endlessly varied combinations.

As in most fields of Renaissance culture, so also in poetry, Italy was first off the mark. That quintessentially medieval poet Dante (1265–1321) was also among the first to show a new awareness of the classics and a new stress on the independent human sensibility. But the first indisputably Renaissance figure—though he did not relinquish his medieval legacy—was Francesco Petrarca or Petrarch (1304–74). Today we prize Petrarch chiefly for his Italian love poetry; but he also wrote a Latin epic, *Africa,* along with other Latin poems and philosophic works. And most fundamentally, he inaugurated what we call Renaissance humanism: the creative study and absorption of classical writings and culture, with the cultivation of moral and philosophic ideals based on them.

In Petrarch's footsteps came Boccaccio, and the next two hundred years saw remarkably rich and sustained poetic activity in

[1] The gradual disuse of Latin has obscured the influence of Renaissance Neo-Latin poetry on the vernacular literature of the age, as also the individual excellence of poets like the Italians Giovanni Pontano, Angelo Poliziano and Jacopo Sannazaro; the Dutch Johannes Secundus; the Scottish George Buchanan; and the Polish Casimir Sarbiewski—to name only some of the finest.

various Italian city-states: Florence, Naples and Ferrara above all, but also Urbino, Padua, Mantua and the papal court at Rome.

The Italian influence bore earliest fruit in Spain, culminating in the 'age of gold' (*siglo d'oro*) of the later sixteenth century. In France, classical and Italian influence first truly comes to flower in the group of poets called the Pléiade, the greatest of them being Pierre de Ronsard.

II. EARLY MODELS AND THEIR TRANSMISSION

In England, after a few abortive starts in the fifteenth century, classical scholarship gained firm footing with a generation of early sixteenth-century humanists, off whom the best known was Sir Thomas More. England also developed one of the best networks of grammar schools of any European country, and Latin poetry formed perhaps the single biggest component of the curriculum. The Latin poetry produced in England was largely mediocre; but a general awareness of classical poetry was built up over the decades. Classical models were followed, often in clumsy ways, in such diverse models as Sir Thomas Wyatt's satires, Alexander Barclay's eclogues, and the epigrams of Wyatt and Robert Crowley.

It is the Italian influence that is most marked in the first really successful productions of the 'new poetry': the sonnets of Wyatt and Surrey, clearly following (and in some cases translating) those of Petrarch; while Wyatt's other poetry shows a more general influence of Petrarch as well as of other Italian poets, especially Serafino Aquilano, Luigi Alamanni and Pietro Aretino.

Apart from the sonnet, Wyatt and Surrey practised the *terza rima*, the *ottava rima* and the *strambotto* out of Italian, and Wyatt the *rondeau* out of French. The same influences, drawn partly from the Latin work of Horace, Catullus and later poets, and partly from Italian sources (gradually augmented by Spanish and French), operate through the less exciting but often suggestive work of mid-sixteenth-century poets and underlie the triumphant creations of the 1580s, the 1590s and the early seventeenth century.

Other poetic forms also appear in the earlier sixteenth century—most notably blank verse, as first used (after Italian models) by the Earl of Surrey around 1540 in his translation of Books II and IV of

Virgil's *Aeneid.* But significant development of long poems and sustained verse-forms came later in the century. The crucial formative stages of the 'new poetry' developed through the lyric.

Printed collections of short poems, both by single authors and in anthologies, appear in the early and mid-sixteenth century. But it bears remembering that such poetry was chiefly disseminated through privately circulated manuscripts. The influence of Italianate Renaissance culture had made poetry a gentlemanly accomplishment, to be composed and read privately in exclusive circles, unsullied by what J.W. Saunders has termed the 'stigma of print'.[2] Many aristocratic poets, beginning with Wyatt amd Surrey, did make their way into print in their own age or soon after. Others (like Sir Arthur Gorges and Sir Robert Sidney, Sir Philip's brother) lay hidden in manuscripts that were discovered only in recent times. New Tudor poets and poems, of varying degrees of importance, come to light every now and then. No doubt there is a rich store waiting to be discovered, though an equal quantity must have been lost for good. Perhaps one day a scholar will stumble on a store of poems by Robert de Vere, Earl of Oxford, or Ferdinando Stanley, Earl of Derby, who are at present little more than names.

Needless to say, print gradually came to triumph as the recognized medium of successful poetry. The change may have been speeded by the publication of Sir Philip Sidney's works after his death by his sister Mary Herbert, Countess of Pembroke. But right through the Tudor age, even professional writers thought it necessary to offer apologies or fictitious explanations for publishing their work. The abundance of dedications to aristocratic patrons also indicates the continuing concept of a more restricted and personalized circulation.

The basic point to note is that Tudor poetry enjoyed a unique range of audience-choice, motives and situations of composition. The leading points of bearing were: circulation in manuscript among equals in the aristocracy, or among educated persons generally in print or manuscript; presentation by commoner-poets, often though not always professional writers, to upper-class patrons; and writing for the new anonymous public created by the printing press. But these were not exclusive choices. Poems written

[2] In the title of an article in *Essays in Criticism*, vol. 1 (1951).

by and for aristocrats could find their way into print, perhaps in the author's despite, to interest a wider audience. A poet could dedicate to one or several patrons (often, though not always, in the hope of direct reward) a work that was coming out in print for public sale.

It was also general practice among educated men of the age to keep private notebooks and 'commonplace books' in which they copied out poems or other matter that had appealed to them in the course of their reading. Such 'manuscript miscellanies' could reach a publisher and be printed as a collection of poems. Or else a publisher might himself gather poems from various sources, manuscript or print, to compile an anthology. Thus there came into being the printed miscellanies which provide important repositories of English Renaissance poetry. The best known (though not, it seems, the earliest) is *Songs and Sonnets*, published in 1557 and known as 'Tottel's Miscellany' after its compiler and publisher, Richard Tottel. This collection preserved Wyatt's and Surrey's poems, among others, for the times to come, though better texts have now been discovered in manuscript. The 1570s and 1580s saw more such collections, and in the next decade came *The Phoenix' Nest* (1593) commemorating Sidney; *The Passionate Pilgrim* (1599) with two sonnets certainly and some other poems possibly by Shakespeare; and the exceptionally fine *England's Helicon* (1600), a collection of pastoral poems.

We also find a substantial body of lyric poetry included in other types of works. The prose narratives of the age yield a good store, most notably Sidney's *Arcadia* and the euphuistic romances of Robert Greene and Thomas Lodge. So does the drama, though such songs and poems (like the plays themselves) found their way into print only occasionally and in unreliable texts. The songs from Shakespeare's plays are well known. Many of Ben Jonson's finest lyrics also belong to his plays, and there are good examples from dramatists as diverse as John Lyly, George Peele, Thomas Dekker, John Webster and Thomas Heywood.

More reliably and substantially, large numbers of lyrics were set to music and printed (with musical notation) in the song-books of the age. I shall speak later of the importance of such musical models for the general form and structure of the lyric.

This account should have conveyed the crucial point that to the Elizabethans poetry was not only something 'read in a book' or cultivated by a handful of eccentrics. The educated man, even the courtier and man of affairs, was fed poetry from many sources: indeed, he practised the art himself and was formally trained to do so. Again, the common man, even if he were illiterate, would imbibe poetry from the plays he saw, the songs he heard, and the broadsheets hawked in fairs and markets. The age's preoccupation with poetry has often been exaggerated and romanticized; but it is a fact that poetry was part of the working consciousness of the average Elizabethan (though the manner may have varied with his social class and education) to an extent unique in English cultural history.

III: 'PLAIN' AND 'COURTLY' POETRY

It is customary to date the 'new poetry' from the time of Wyatt and Surrey. But it was an uncertain start. Up to the 1580s the new spirit competed closely with older strains and models; and even afterwards the presence of the latter was strongly felt. Indeed, the two veins cannot be clearly separated: as may be expected, they blend and interact, and are best regarded as the two ends of a spectrum of possibilities along which individual poems and poets range themselves. It is risky to talk in terms of 'old' and 'new' at all; still more in value-loaded terms like 'drab' or 'golden' as proposed by C.S. Lewis.[3] Yet any student of Elizabethan poetry comes to discern the interplay of two elements or tendencies, compatible and indeed complementary but basically opposite in purport, and one more innovative than the other.

The bolder and more eye-catching strain consists chiefly in closer adherence to classical and new continental models; more lively and innovative versification; new themes and concerns, even new philosophies (such as Neo-Platonism) generated by the Renaissance; and a new vein of diction and composition, exploiting the fresh resources of vocabulary and more prone to rhetorical ornament. The staider, quieter vein prefers old-fashioned poetic forms; it is more rigid in verse-movement and conservative in diction; its

[3] C.S. Lewis, *English Literature in the Sixteenth Century (Excluding Drama)*, Oxford History of English Literature (Oxford, 1954), pp. 64–5, 478–83. The book has now been reissued as *Poetry and Prose in the Sixteenth Century*.

themes tend towards the openly moral and didactic, or at most to a few set uses of conventions (such as Petrarchism) that had since evolved new and more sophisticated forms. This type of poetry forgoes both the virtues and the vices of ornamental figures of speech; its greater simplicity induces a more apparent logical structure.

Perhaps the best terms proposed to define these contrary veins are Yvor Winters's 'plain' and 'courtly'; but few are likely to share Winters's marked preference for the former, among whose exponents he places Wyatt, Ralegh and Jonson.[4] As a matter of fact, Wyatt's poetry introduces 'courtly' innovation into English poetry. The 'plain' element dominates in Gascoigne, Turberville and the less-known Thomas Howell; but their moderate success lies precisely in that they use newer themes and models to extend the possibilities of basically simple, conservative verse-forms and diction. Where such modification is absent (as, say, in Barnabe Googe) even the formal adherence to new themes and models proves futile.

The profoundest interaction of old and new occurs in the poetry of Edmund Spenser. His *The Shepherd's Calendar* (1579) inaugurates the full and assured sway of the 'new poetry'; but it incorporates moral themes in explicit allegiance to Chaucer, Langland and their followers, and makes extensive use of archaic diction and rough-cut verse-forms. Again, *The Faerie Queene* (1590)—one of the greatest romantic epics of the Renaissance, with remarkable extensions of Renaissance Neo-Platonism through the complex iconography evolved by the age—is also one of the high points of the medieval mode of moral allegory, conveyed through deliberately archaized diction. And we must remember that *The Faerie Queene* was rivalled in popularity by *A Mirror for Magistrates*, a work in the typically medieval tradition of 'the falls of princes', though the moralizing is touched in some contributors by a new intenser interest in psychological states. In diction, imagery and above all versification, the *Mirror* marks some important achievements and experiments. A comparison between the *Mirror* and *The Faerie Queene* is instructive in showing how the 'old' and 'new' veins run close to, and into, each other.

[4] See Winters's essay 'Poetic Styles, Old and New' in D.C. Allen (ed.), *Four Poets on Poetry* (Baltimore, 1959), pp. 44–75.

The innovative achievement of Elizabethan poetry can be roughly grouped under four heads: (a) prosody, (b) diction or vocabulary, (c) rhetorical ordering, and (d) the incorporation of new themes, genres and models. Let us take a closer look at each of these aspects in turn.

IV: PROSODY

Middle English prosody is a complex and bewildering field; but in Chaucer, Gower and a body of late medieval lyrics, we find a close approximation to the standard patterns of later English verse with its systematic ordering of syllables and accents. As I said earlier, the radical changes in the English sound-system in the fifteenth century rendered the scansion of Chaucer's poetry almost incomprehensible. The Chaucerians and the more old-fashioned of the early Tudor poets write in an irregular and undirected manner—or else, like John Skelton, with a brilliantly original but limited and unpromising device, the brief rough-cut 'Skeltonic' verse with its variable syllable-count and tumbling stream of rhymes.

> These serpents of Libany
> Might sting thee venomously.
> The dragons with their tongues
> Might poison thy liver and lungs.
> The manticores of the mountains
> Might feed them on thy brains.
> Melanchates that hound
> That plucked Actaeon to the ground,
> Gave him his mortal wound,
> Changed to a deer,
> The story doth appear
> Was changed to a hart . . . (*Philip Sparrow*)

Elsewhere, these poets seem to be limping towards modern prosody without successfully mastering it. Wyatt's sonnets, as preserved in the best manuscripts, seem at first reading to make clumsy halting sallies at the iambic pentameter:

> She that me learneth to love and suffer

And will that my trust and lust's negligence
Be reined by reason, shame and reverence,
With his hardiness taketh displeasure. (Poem 1 below)

Tottel, when he prints the poems in his miscellany, radically revises them to smooth out the metre. But during the same years, Wyatt was writing other lyrics that scan precisely and indeed with élan. Obviously, the irregular scansion of the sonnets marks a deliberate attempt at a subtler verse-movement, reflecting the exact turns of the poet's thought. It is the result of sophisticated experiment, not ineptitude or lack of norms. The same may be said later of Spenser's innovations in *The Shepherd's Calendar*.

We may of course view Wyatt's experiments not as proceeding on an established metrical base, but as one tentative development of an as yet uncertain prosody. Be that as it may, this prosody, based on stress and syllable-count, soon becomes the norm in a remarkable reaffirmation of Chaucer's metrics. The basic unit is the iambic foot, particularly as in the iambic pentameter. But from the outset, this interacts with other metrical units and principles, some of them deriving from medieval alliterative verse. Among these are a marked half-line division indicated by a pause or caesura:

What have we then to vaunt, / or glory in,
Sith all is vain, / wherein we take delight?
Why should we boast or brag, / sith nought we win
In fine, but death, / to whom yields every wight?
(from *A Gorgeous Gallery of Gallant Inventions*, 1578)

extensive variation in the number of unstressed syllables in a line:

The wearied mind straight from the heart departeth
For to rest in his worldly paradise . . .
Thus is it in such extremity brought:
In frozen thought now, and now it standeth in flame,
'Twixt misery and wealth, 'twixt earnest and game,
But few glad, and many a diverse thought . . .
(Wyatt, Sonnet: 'Advising the bright beams')

above all, the awareness of a basic four-beat movement in any line of English verse even if it is formally pentametric or five-foot:

The long love that in my thought doth harbour

And in mine heart doth keep his residence,
Into my face presseth with bold pretence,
And therein campeth, spreading his banner.
(Poem I below)

The greatest achievement of Elizabethan verse was to incorporate these creative irregularities: by increasingly intricate and sensitive manipulation of pauses, variant feet, run-on lines, varying numbers of syllables with greater or lesser frequency of stresses—all of which modulate the speed and weight of the line. And beneath all these devices is the realization that successful prosody consists in playing off the metrical norm against the pattern of common speech. This perception first appears clearly in Gascoigne's *Certain Notes of Instruction Concerning the Making of Verse or Rhyme in English* (1575).

The new prosody also contributed to the adoption of a wide range of stanza-forms. The seven-line Chaucerian stanza or 'rime royal' (so called from its use by James I of Scotland in *The King's Quire*) was as popular in the sixteenth as in the fourteenth century, and new forms like the nine-line Spenserian stanza were devised by elaborating on the same models. There arose an endless series of new lyric stanza-forms, often based on classical and continental example but harmonized with English prosody and phonology. Most widespread of these was, of course, the sonnet, originally Italian but naturalized all over western Europe. Others include such well-known but ill-defined models as the classical ode, epistle, eclogue and satire and Italian *canzone*; or more rigid, often artificial and intricate forms like the French *balade* and Italian *sestina, dizain, sixain* or *corona*. Many of the terms are used very vaguely in English. 'Sonnet' could mean any love-lyric; so could 'ballad' (vulgarized from French *balade*) even while in another direction the word 'ballad' retained its original sense of a long narrative poem of popular origin. Other terms like 'elegy' meant in Greek or Latin a poem in a particular metre; the terms passed into English (and other European languages) where obviously the metrical effect could not be replicated. Thus the terms came to acquire a new significance: elegy, for instance, has become specifically a poem of lament. There were also attempts at 'quantitative' verse—that is, verse relying as in Greek or Latin on the pattern of long and short syllables. This produced many ingenious pieces and a few memorable ones (like

'O sweet woods . . . ' in Sidney's *Arcadia*) but obviously there could be no future for a verse-principle so remote from the phonetic structure of the English language.

In course of the Elizabethan age, English verse became a supremely suggestive, receptive medium, responding to every slight hint or pressure from a skilful poet's hands. And with this there grew a pervasive sense, perhaps not so widespread or so innately and spontaneously present ever before or since, of sheer vigour and delight in the command of verse. This again can be overstressed or romanticized; but it is palpably present in even the mediocre verse of the age, a happy energy that leavens the presentation of the most conventional as well as the most complex and challenging themes.

V: VOCABULARY AND DICTION

Innovations in vocabulary are even harder to treat briefly. I can only indicate the main directions in which the Tudor poets could avail of an exciting new store of words.

One of the most obvious sources was the stock of Latin borrowings provided by the revival of classical learning. It is estimated that some 10,000 new words entered English from Latin in the sixteenth century. Many of these go back to Greek, and there was a fair measure of direct borrowing from Greek as well. In addition, large numbers of Latin words were absorbed through French or Italian, languages deriving from Latin. French loans had of course been plentiful ever since the Norman Conquest of 1066; but Italian loans entered English in large numbers only in the sixteenth century, partly through English travellers to Italy, but more commonly through the new interest in Italian literature.

The ever-alert Tudor critics were quick to brand excessive or misguided use of these new resources as 'inkhorn terms' (pedantic Latin loans) and 'oversea language' (from the continental vernaculars). With them they coupled the abuse of a third rich resource, 'Chaucerisms'—i.e. conscious archaisms drawn from Chaucer and other Middle English poetry, or sometimes inauthentic forms coined on their analogy. We cannot always tell what would have counted as an archaism in the Elizabethan age and what, obsolete to us, might then have been current. But in most cases, philologists know the answer; and in any case, archaizing effects are often too obvious to miss. *The Shepherd's Calendar* affords the classic case:

Hobbinoll. Diggon Davie, I bid her good day:
Or Diggon it is, or I missay.

Diggon. Her was her, while it was daylight;
But now her is a most wretched wight.
For day, that was, is wightly past,
And now at erst the dark night doth haste.

Hobbinoll. Diggon areed, who has thee so dight?
Never I wist thee in so poor a plight.
('September' ll.1–8)

It may not be the word itself that is archaic, but a prefix like *y-* or *be-*, a suffix like *-en* after plural verbs, or unfamiliar forms and usages. Archaizing affixes mark a special case of a general feature of Tudor English—the ease with which new compounds could be formed by freely drawing upon a floating stock of affixes. Some of the words so formed have survived, others not, apparently by the caprice of chance. Many such compounds, no doubt, were nonce-words not meant to last. So doubtless were many of the bolder compounds formed by running together two stem-words or even whole phrases: Sidney's 'long-with-love-acquainted', 'young-wise, wise-valiant' and 'mark-wanting shafts'; Spenser's 'broad-blazed', 'after-send', 'groundhold' (anchor), 'bellibone' (French *belle et bonne*, 'pretty and good'); Donne's 'through-shine' (transparent), 'winter-seeming', 'tear-floods' and 'sigh-tempests'; Shakespeare's 'high-gravel-blind, 'the be-all and the end-all' and 'world-without-end hour'.[5]

This brings us to the crucial feature of the new Elizabethan vocabulary—I may say the new Elizabethan approach to the language generally. More than any age since, and probably before, the Elizabethans regarded words not as fixed units to accept and apply passively but as a fluid, expanding, infinitely permutable fund of

[5] See respectively Sidney, *Astrophil and Stella* 31.5, 75.5, 99.3; Spenser, *The Faerie Queene* I.x.11, I.v.10, *The Shepherd's Calendar* 'April' 92; Donne, 'Valediction: of My Name in the Window' 8, 'Love's Alchemy' 12, 'Valediction: Forbidding Mourning' 6; Shakespeare, *The Merchant of Venice* II.ii.34, *Macbeth* I.vii.5, Sonnet 57.5.

material—components rather than fully-cast forms—that any intelligent user could work creatively, the poet or 'maker' above all. Even second-ranking Elizabethan poets frequently give this impression of shaping and drawing out the language; and a Spenser, a Donne or a Shakespeare virtually creates his language as he goes along in a perceptible, at times flamboyant way that comparable poets do not in later ages.

This language-making on the poet's part also shows in the way he manipulates the unprecedentedly rich and varied vocabulary at his disposal. He can concentrate on a particular resource—archaisms in Spenser, Latinisms in Milton—to create a special effect. Or, with a subtler skill, he can shift from one type of diction to another, or interweave them in a finely attuned texture: in Shakespeare's famous

multitudinous seas incarnadine
Making the green one red.

(*Macbeth* II.ii.61–2)

or, say, in Spenser's

Tell me, have ye seen her angelic face,
Like Phoebe fair?
Her heavenly haviour, her princely grace
Can you well compare?
The red rose meddled with the white y-fere,
In either cheek depeinten lively cheer.

(*The Shepherd's Calendar*, 'April' ll.64–9)

VI: RHETORIC

In this control of the new word-treasure he has won, the Elizabethan poet is guided—again, more than any English poet before or since—by the principles of classical rhetoric as modified by the humanism of the age. Poetics was then a nascent line of enquiry; it was rhetoric, a discipline extensively developed in ancient Greece and Rome, that guided all use of language, including poetry. The Latin rhetorical treatises of Cicero and Quintilian were generally studied; they were backed by Hermogenes and Aphthonius in Greek (read in Renaissance schools in Latin translation) and the *Rhetorica ad Herennium* (thought to be by Cicero) in Latin.

There was also an endless stream of new works based on these, perhaps adapted to the modern languages. In English, the most important of these were Thomas Wilson's *The Art of Rhetoric* (1553) and Abraham Fraunce's *The Arcadian Rhetoric* (1584).

It is hard for us to recapture the crucial role of rhetoric in guiding both composition and appreciation of poetry in the Renaissance. We cannot share the commentator E.K.'s delight in a passage from *The Shepherd's Calendar* because of 'its pretty Epanorthosis in these two verses, and withal a Paranomasia or playing with the word'. This hunt for figures of speech was indeed the outermost manifestation of the rhetorical consciousness. To us, 'rhetoric' chiefly implies ornate or elaborate language. To the Elizabethans, such embellishments of speech were indeed important, and the new poetry shows a marked increase in their use. But adornment or 'locution' was the last stage in a process that began with the basic conception ('invention') and structuring ('disposition') of the piece. The ordering of the parts was crucial; equally so the determination of the nature of the piece and the appropriate type or level of language. The 'doctrine of kinds' was a basic literary concept of the age; and the 'kind' to which a work belonged—whether epic, tragedy, ode, comedy, satire or pastoral, to name a few—determined the appropriate language, graded along a three-part categorizing of 'high', 'mean' (middle) and 'low' styles. To maintain this 'decorum' was the poet's fundamental duty to his craft.

Rhetorical figures and principles of composition need not obtrude; nor need they be applied with a deadening hand. The light unreflecting joy of a brief song-lyric represents a rhetorical decision, an application of the doctrine of kinds, no less than the epic sweep and 'grand style' of *Paradise Lost*. Rhetorical patterns and tropes are as apparent in the seemingly disordered, spontaneous flow of Donne's poems or the soliloquies of Shakespeare's tragic heroes as in the declamations of didactic poets. Rhetoric is indeed nothing but a systematization of the natural, untutored principles of effective expression. The Elizabethans were unusually successful in naturalizing it to meet their deepest aesthetic demands.

Books have been written on the niceties of Elizabethan prosody, diction and rhetoric. In my notes, I have pointed out some specially important occurrences; but obviously, it is for the reader to respond to the endless play of local effects in all these spheres. I can only alert him to their importance.

In the same way, I cannot expatiate on the doctrine of kinds, or give an exhaustive account of the genres, themes and conventions of Elizabethan poetry. In what follows, I shall merely provide the background for studying some important types as contained in this representative selection.

VII: THEMES, GENRES AND MODELS

(a) ***The Pastoral***: The genre on which young poets were conventionally advised to cut their teeth was the pastoral—on the model of Virgil, whose Latin Eclogues or pastoral poems were probably his earliest work. Virgil was following the Greek Theocritus (third century B.C.), who, on surviving evidence, began this mode of poetry presenting the lives of idealized shepherds in an aesthetically ordered landscape. Theocritus' shepherds are not too strongly idealized; the creation of an idyllic Arcadia begins with Virgil, or rather with the later accentuation of certain traits in Virgil's varied work. Virgil also started, and his imitators extended, the practice of using fictional shepherds as allegorical masks for real persons. In the Middle Ages and the Renaissance, the bulk of pastoral poetry contains allusions to, or allegories of, politics, church affairs, the poets' own lives, or other external events. The pastoral fiction grows conventional and perfunctory, and sometimes virtually disappears. But a more memorable vein of pastoral preserves the imaginative setting of a peaceful, harmonious, truly simple world—sometimes unreal and sentimentalized, but at its best profound and imaginative, of unusual purity and intensity.

Pastoral is not really a genre; rather, it is an imaginative mode. Its established vehicle is the eclogue, a fairly short poem of indeterminate form, often incorporating set monologues, dialogues or song-contests. There is a single Greek pastoral romance, *Daphnis and Chloe*, from late classical times (second–third century A.D.). The Renaissance virtually created the forms of pastoral romance and pastoral drama—first, as usual, in Italy, spreading thence to Spain, France and England in particular. Such works may present courtiers alongside shepherds, or the latter alone; the pastoral setting may dominate the work or only provide an interlude. These extended pastoral narratives provide some of the profoundest and most suggestive versions of the mode. But more often than not, they have inset eclogues and lyrics; English poetry in particular affords a remarkably fine range of short pastoral lyrics, briefer, more varied and more delicate than the eclogue. These were expertly collected in the anthology *England's Helicon* (1600).

(b) ***Sonnets and Other Love Poetry***: 'And then the lover, sighing like furnace.' Perhaps the best-known type of Renaissance poetry is the love-poem, particularly the sonnet, as epitomized in the work of Francesco Petrarca or Petrarch (1304–74). The standard features of this vein of love-poetry are the worshipful adoration of an idealized mistress and a sense of the elevating, even spiritualizing function of love. The line can be traced back to the troubadours of southern France from the twelfth to the fourteenth centuries, and even to certain Arabic influences transmitted via Spain. Its first full-fledged expression is in Italian (chiefly Florentine) poets of the thirteenth and early fourteenth centuries, who achieve perhaps the most emphatic expression of the refining and spiritualizing influence of love. In Dante's *La Vita Nuova* ('The New Life'), a sonnet-sequence linked by prose commentary, the poet's love of Beatrice becomes a means of attaining to the divine. But it is Petrarch who, combining this spiritual quest with secular and psychological themes, provides the classic model for European love-poetry for the next three hundred years and more.

Petrarch's love for Laura is inspired by her exceptional virtue as well as beauty and grace; the poet is led towards enlightenment, virtue and heaven itself. At the same time, this very virtue in the beloved fills the lover with shame and frustration at the basic carnality of his love and the impossibility of his attaining to one so perfect. He retreats to solitary nature and laments his woes to the mountains, rivers and trees. At other moments again, he is moved by a more erotic passion—the sight or the very thought of his mistress's beauty.

Elements from this unprecedentedly rich and demanding compound provide the staple of Renaissance love-poetry; but as might be expected, few poets attain to Petrarch's depth and subtlety. The bulk of Petrarchan poetry consists of hackneyed effusions of sentimental lovers. However, gifted poets can introduce charm and a measure of novelty even into these conventionalities. Others can extend Petrarchan convention by recourse to other traditions or philosophies, especially the spiritualizing power of Neo-Platonism. Or they might modify Petrarchan idealism by drawing on classical models like Catullus' lyrics and Ovid's love-elegies, with their candid ardour and at times open eroticism. Although Petrarchan love-convention was often reduced to a narrow repertoire of stereotypes, it was essentially a varied and challenging mode: above all, an open-ended one that allowed free incorporation of new themes and models. It provided one of the most fertile and dynamic bodies of poetry in the age, perhaps reaching its highest points in the sonnets of Michelangelo and Shakespeare.

Petrarchism finds expression through many mediums: romance, drama, philosophic discourse, and various forms of lyric. But its most particular vehicle is the sonnet, which arose in thirteenth-century Italy more or less concurrently with the new love-poetry and in association with it. Dante, his predecessors and contemporaries use it extensively; 318 of Petrarch's 366 *Rime* are sonnets, and the classic Italian sonnet-form has been named after him. The Petrarchan sonnet has an octave, eight lines rhyming *abba abba*, followed by a sestet whose six lines can rhyme more freely, except that they never conclude with a couplet. There is commonly a *volta* or 'turn' between octava and sestet. But this scheme is often modified, especially in England, where, beginning with the innovation of a concluding couplet, there gradually evolves the 'English' or 'Shakespearean' sonnet rhyming *abab cdcd efef gg*. This form is predominant (but not universal) in the Elizabethan age. In later centuries, poets alternate between the Italian and English schemes.

Dante had his Beatrice and Petrarch his Laura. Often since then, love-sonnets have been composed in sequences telling—or at least reflecting—the story of a love-affair, more often than not based on an actual one in the poet's life. The first English sonnets, by Wyatt and Surrey, are not, however, sequences, though Surrey's deal occasionally with his love for 'Geraldine' (a matter much exaggerated by sentimental commentators), and some of Wyatt's also appear autobiographical. Elizabethan poets commonly wrote their love-sonnets in cycles or sequences. Sidney's *Astrophil and Stella* reflects his love for Penelope Devereux before and after she married another man. Spenser's *Amoretti* traces his courtship of his future wife, Elizabeth Boyle, culminating in an 'Epithalamion' or marriage song. Drayton's *Idea* celebrates his patroness Anne Goodere, for whom he may or may not have felt a distant worshipful adoration. Shakespeare's sonnets famously record the course of a cryptic triangular relationship between the poet, an aristocratic 'Friend' and a 'Dark Lady'.

As will be obvious from these prominent examples, the nature of the relationship varies widely, and may indeed use love-convention as the poetic vehicle for what is not basically a love-relationship at all. Even when there is an obvious reflection of the poet's personal life, we need not take every detail and episode as authentic biography. We should be still more cautious about reading narrative or chronological sequences into a cycle. *Astrophil and Stella* proves on dispassionate reading not to yield any clear story of thwarted love; and the story of Shakespeare's alleged loves is notoriously controversial. Rather than speculate pruriently upon these matters, it is better to read the sonnet-cycle as an independent narrative, often challengingly oblique in method. More basically, the Elizabethan love-sonnet affords our readiest access to Renaissance perceptions of love—a uniquely rich body of thoughts and attitudes, that for the first time establish love in its modern perspective as a governing factor in human life.

(c) *Song-poetry*: Besides the sonnet, Petrarchan love found expression in a variety of lyrics, ranging from the substantial, often completely meditative *canzone* to delicate song-like pieces. But nearly all Renaissance lyrics are closely allied to song. There is an important area of Renaissance poetry operating under the dual control of words and music.

Folk music flourished in the Middle Ages alongside courtly music. In the Tudor age, the latter gained ground in an expanding range of court functions and entertainments. Formally too, it gained in sophistication through new harmonizing techniques from the continent. The most significant consequence was the rise of the madrigal or 'partsong', with several voices in harmony. The 'air' was a simpler melodic performance, usually solo and sung to the lute. The Elizabethan age saw a steady stream of song-books, both 'airs' and 'madrigals'. The composers included William Byrd (1543–1623), John Dowland (1563–1626), Thomas Morley (1557–1602) and Thomas Campion (1567–1620). The words were sometimes written by the composers: Campion, for instance, is equally notable as poet and as musician. Other pieces might have words by well-known poets of the day. In yet other cases, the authorship is unknown.

Musically complex songs can be verbally sparse, though many pieces in these song-books are remarkable for their poetic content. The chief point of interest, however, is not the actual song-lyric but the bulk of other Elizabethan lyrics, not set to music yet with a marked song-like quality, a limpid movement that may or may not follow an accepted musical structure. We often cannot tell which poems are formally 'songs' and which are not. The way musical forms have left their mark on the distinct medium of language is perhaps the most remarkable feature of these poems. Their diction is also commonly light, simple, colloquial—but passing by degrees into the stylized, artificial or affected. Folk-song and courtly song merge undetectably here, supported by the background presence of medieval lyric models with their own fusions of the popular and the courtly.

Through its deceptively light, transparent medium, the Elizabethan lyric traces all the serious concerns of classical lyric and pastoral; of Petrarchan love-poetry and the new late-medieval awareness of nature; and philosophic themes, points of Neo-Platonism for instance, alongside touches of Christian spiritual meditation.

(d) *The Romantic Epic*: Needless to say, the Renaissance also abounded in longer poetic forms. Foremost among these was the romantic epic—long, intricate tales of love, adventure and the supernatural, based on the twin models of classical epic and medieval romance. Elements of the latter usually dominate, with the accent on the romantic and the marvellous. This is raised to an intense and graceful pitch of imagination, and at the same time modulated by a humorous tempering of its own excess of fancy, in Lodovico Ariosto's *Orlando Furioso* ('The Mad Orlando', 1516). But there soon arose a counter-tendency towards more intellective, patriotic or spiritual subjects, seen at its finest in Torquato Tasso's *Gerusalemme Liberata* ('Jerusalem Delivered', finished 1575, published 1581), a story of the Crusades that acquires true epic grandeur. Ariosto's poem was translated by Sir John Harington in 1591, Tasso's by Edward Fairfax in 1600, though educated Elizabethans would be familiar with the Italian originals.

This was the legacy which Spenser put to use in *The Faerie Queene*. Spenser's originality lies in combining romantic narrative with not only serious themes but explicit allegory in the medieval manner. The chief knight in each book is associated with a particular virtue: Holiness, Temperance, Chastity, Friendship, Justice, Courtesy. They all serve Queen Gloriana—'glory' in general as well as Elizabeth of England—and are aided by Prince Arthur, who symbolizes Christian grace among other things. The subsidiary characters are usually allegorical in some way, though seldom bald personifications. At times the allegory can be conventionally moral or doctrinally Christian; elsewhere, however, it embodies Platonic or other philosophic concepts of a type generated in the Renaissance, conveyed through distinctively Renaissance redactions of classical myth or more esoteric 'mysteries' drawn from other ancient cultures. There is moreover a good deal of political allegory.

It is Spenser's achievement to present this mighty and intricate range of concerns through a narrative that holds us sometimes by the sheer excitement of events, and continually by vivid, evocative descriptions and an endless flow of mythic imagination. These qualities are so compelling, and so readily accessible even to a casual reader of short extracts, that they may distract us from the deeper intellectual challenges of *The Faerie Queene*. Only extensive reading can reveal the fascinating design of this poem which, more than any other single work, brings together the literary and philosophic legacy of the late Middle Ages and the Renaissance. An anthology like this has to be content with representative episodes and descriptions.[6]

(e) ***The Short Epic***: Needless to say, romance, myth and didactic or philosophic material provide matter for other types of poetry, separately or in simpler combinations. Myth, love story and exoticism

[6] Later poets—including declared Spenserians such as Michael Drayton, Giles and Phineas Fletcher, William Browne and George Wither—could follow Spenser's model only in part. The most ambitious attempt was perhaps William Browne's unfinished *Britannia's Pastorals* (Book I 1613, Book II 1616), which applies Spenser's mode of allegorical romance to pastoral material. But *The Faerie Queene* remains unique.

are combined memorably in the epyllion or 'short epic'. The Greek poet Apollonius of Rhodes (third century B.C.) provided the model in his *Argonautica*, but the chief inspiration came from the Latin work of Ovid (43 B.C.–A.D. 18). The mythic stories, and something of the charged mythic atmosphere, derive from Ovid's *Metamorphoses*; the frank eroticism, humour and exuberance from his *Amores* or love-elegies. Shakespeare's *Venus and Adonis* and Marlowe's *Hero and Leander* provide the finest instances of the English epyllion; but Thomas Lodge's *Scilla's Metamorphosis* (1589), Drayton's *Endimion and Phebe* (1595), John Weever's *Faunus and Melliflora* (1600) and Francis Beaumont's *Salmacis and Hermaphroditus* (1602) testify equally to the revitalization of classical myth in that age, so prominent in the synthesis of *The Faerie Queene*.

(f) ***Satire and Didactic Poetry***: Much more numerous are the various types of satiric and didactic poetry. Classical poetry provided two main models of satire: witty and genial in Horace, more bitter and sombre in Juvenal and Persius. As usual in such cases, the two are best regarded as interacting tendencies rather than as black-and-white alternatives, though Elizabethan satirists commonly classified their work as either Horatian or Juvenalian, 'toothless' or 'biting' in Joseph Hall's phrase. Nor was satire confined to classical models, needless to say. Skelton wrote some witty, imaginative and hard-hitting satires in his distinctive style, and there was a whole line of poetry drawing on the social satire so prominent in that complex fourteenth-century visionary work, William Langland's *Piers Plowman*. In classical-type satire, Wyatt again provides the first notable instances, specifically on Italian models; but the type came into its own about the turn of the century in the work of John Donne, Joseph Hall and John Marston. The subtle thought, penetration and genuine humanity of Donne's satires make them particularly appealing even to the modern reader.

We may find it more difficult to respond to the didactic, moral and philosophic poetry that abounded in that age, as in most others down to the nineteenth century. Some of this consists of relatively short pieces, like Spenser's *Four Hymns* (1596) that together provide the finest poetic exposition of Christian Neo-Platonism in English. But most didactic and discursive poems tend to be long. In a class of its own is Drayton's *Poly-Olbion* (1612, 1622), which we may fitly call a descriptive epic. It is a comprehensive survey of British history and geography, region by region. What might have been an arid succession of facts becomes in Drayton's hands a rich tapestry of stirring historical narrative, occasional satire, vivid nature-description, above all a sustained vein of myth-making that transforms the English countryside into a timeless living reality like the landscapes of classical poetry, Drayton's economy is remarkable: *Poly-Olbion* is a long poem in thirty 'Songs', but individual descriptions and episodes are drawn with a minimum of skilful strokes.

More common didactic themes may also be treated in original or fanciful vein, as in George Chapman's obscure philosophic fantasies, *The Shadow of Night* (1594) and *Ovid's Banquet of Sense* (1595) or, later, Phineas Fletcher's *The Purple Island* (1633), a curious allegory of man's physical and mental composition. The same subject had been treated simply and directly in Sir John Davies's *Nosce Teipsum* ('Know Yourself', 1599); and Davies's *Orchestra* (1596) provides a happy blend of lucid philosophizing and graceful poetic fancy. The metaphor of music is applied, at level after level, to the harmonies of human nature and the universe. E.M.W. Tillyard took *Orchestra* as an epitome of the 'Elizabethan World Picture'. That may be going too far, but this relatively obscure poem provides an attractive version of a basic Elizabethan concept of the world.

I have given above only a brief survey of the important poetic types represented in this book. It obviously excludes many other significant genres: the verse-epistle, for instance, or the epigram. Also, my account covers chiefly the orthodox forms as cultivated by the literary establishment or upper, educated classes of society. Drawing partly upon these, but very different in its total content, purpose and impact, is an extensive range of songs, ballads, satires and narrative poems, as well as moral and religious pieces, circulated orally and through crudely printed broadsheets. The impact of these extended to the illiterate population. There was also a modest but perceptible influence in the opposite direction, formal or 'literary' verse consciously adopting popular and 'folk' effects.

VII: SOME MAJOR POETS

It is crucial to consider Elizabethan poetry in terms of genres, currents and conventions rather than individual poets. What distinguishes this period above all others is the *collective* cultivation of poetry, so that particular poets—though strongly individual in place of the true anonymity of the Middle Ages—take their places within a movement greater than themselves. They initiate or develop traditions, and ultimately these traditions define the age. Elizabethan poets—in contrast to, say, the Romantics—saw themselves as working within a well-defined system of genres and conventions.

(a) ***Spenser***: Still, a few figures tower over the scene. The most individual among them is Edmund Spenser (1552–99), though he perhaps absorbed more poetic tradition in his work than any of his compeers. He was introduced to court circles in his youth, and associated with Sir Philip Sidney at the house of the latter's uncle, the Earl of Leicester. In *The Shepherd's Calendar* (1579) he virtually inaugurated not merely Renaissance English pastoral but the effective reign of the 'new poetry'; and with mild reservations, Sidney lauded the new (as yet anonymous) poet in his *Apology for Poetry*. The *Calendar* was also Spenser's conscious inauguration of a planned poetic career. No earlier English poet had projected and yet transformed his own poetic personality as Spenser did in the figure of Colin the shepherd-poet. In a series of minor works, collected in *Complaints* (1591), he opened up English poetry as never before to a number of conventional genres; produced one of the finest English sonnet cycles in *Amoretti*; and showed how the medium-length poem could be adopted to either grandeur of tone and form, as in the marriage songs 'Prothalamion' and 'Epithalamion', or to a rarer philosophic elevation, in the *Four Hymns*.

Spenser's search for court preferment had the disconcerting result of sending him to Ireland for the best years of his life: a cultural exile, enlivened only by a small circle of kindred spirits and occasional trips to London. Yet *The Faerie Queene* might never have been composed had Spenser not been faced with this enforced leisure and total reliance on his own poetic enterprise, as well as a profound imaginative engagement with the Irish landscape.

I have said earlier that Spenser had no true successors; but there was a circle of declared Spenserian poets, and the profound influence of his poetry is apparent in the earlier seventeenth century and again in the eighteenth and nineteenth, in the Romantics and their precursors. He has contributed a depressing amount to the much-abused conventional 'poetic diction'; but even this testifies to the influence of the 'poet's poet'.

(b) ***Sidney***: Influential in a still more radical way was Sir Philip Sidney (1554–86). His corpus (especially of verse) is much smaller; and needless to say, this sparkling, if somewhat peripheral and variable young luminary at Elizabeth's court had no intention of pursuing a poetic career as his life's chief goal. The large, often experimental body of verse included in his prose romance *Arcadia* shows great skill and imagination, but remains curiously directionless. His reputation as poet rests chiefly on his sonnet-sequence *Astrophil and Stella*. But his real importance lies elsewhere. Through his remarkably intensive contact with the cream of European intellectual life, as built up through several triumphant visits to the continent, it was he who brought to England not merely the standard critical theories but the vital poetic spirit of the age. His theories (as enshrined in *The Apology for Poetry*) belong to the seminal but, in England, uneasy line of neo-classicism. His more fundamental contribution is a new facility in exploring complex verse-forms and, more deeply, a language charged with new immediacy and humanity.

As the Elizabethan age settled into a sustained period of productivity, the lead (at least as we see it) passed from poetry to drama. But it must be remembered that drama was commonly regarded in that age as a doubtful and impure literary medium, an ephemeral and populist product: its texts were freely revisable and, in any case, subject to distortion in performance. The notional lead remained with non-dramatic poetry, though some of its finest exponents were dramatists as well. Of Shakespeare's sonnets and long poems I need not speak; nor of Marlowe with his unfinished *Hero and Leander*. The respect in which Ben Jonson was held rested less on his plays than on his scholarship and critical authority, and the remarkable synthesis of disciplined form with grace of utterance in his slender corpus of poetry.

(c) ***Drayton***: Of the wholly non-dramatic poets, John Donne (and the later Metaphysicals) lie outside the purview of this book. There is another crucial figure, perhaps the most neglected of the great

Elizabethans: Michael Drayton (1563–1631). A professed Spenserian, Drayton outdid his master in the range of forms he practised: pastorals, sonnets, historical poems, satires, epistles, ballads, hymns, as well as the monumental *Poly-Olbion.* Amazingly, he subjected this huge body of writing to continuous revision. An admirably serious, dedicated, balanced and modest worker, he seems to have been widely liked and respected in literary circles, but to have withdrawn more and more in spirit to a retreat of his own imagination.

This was not simply escapism: it was a reaction to the times. Increasing dissatisfaction with James's reign was creating political currents that would culminate in the Civil War of the 1640s. This was reflected in the open satire and comment of many poets, including the younger Spenserians such as George Wither and William Browne. But it also found expression in nostalgic evocation of Elizabeth's reign and the principles she was now said (not always correctly) to have stood for. Drayton links this Elizabethan nostalgia to poetic history, and creates in his last pastoral work, *The Muses' Elysium,* an enchanted world enshrining that hardy myth, the 'Elizabethan Golden Age'.

In the foregoing account, I have often hinted that we should not naïvely accept this idea of a 'golden age'. The Elizabethan period had much that was disturbing and disordered, grim, sordid or unheroic. Its poetry is a bewildering mixture of contrary elements. It is not even 'Elizabethan' in a simple chronological sense. Yet there remains an overriding sense of energy, innovation and creative zest, of the poets' participation in a 'common pursuit'. More than in any other age (except perhaps the twentieth century), a crowd of significant poets gather round the giants: flamboyant, original spirits like Robert Greene and Thomas Lodge; more sober careerists like Samuel Daniel; skilful lyricists from Nicholas Breton to Robert Herrick or the still later Cavalier poets, chief among them being Robert Lovelace and John Suckling; weighty intellectual presences like George Chapman and Fulke Greville, Sidney's friend and biographer. The Metaphysicals, of course, make up the most substantial poetic presence in the first half of the seventeenth century; and Milton had commenced his career by 1630.

Milton is of the Renaissance in the best sense; but he is not

'Elizabethan'. He represents a more exacting method and ethos of composition—partly born of his unique self, but partly a sign of new developments. Neo-classicism was about to bear its peculiarly English fruits at last. A broader, more easy-flowing poetic current had come to an end.

IX: FURTHER READING

The best way to understand English Renaissance poetry is to read as much of it as possible. The lyric poetry has been gathered in a number of anthologies, the most comprehensive being Norman Ault's *Elizabethan Lyrics* (revised edition, New York, 1949) and the *Oxford Books* of *Sixteenth* and *Seventeenth-Century Verse* (1932, 1934). Other useful collections are Edward Lucie-Smith's *Penguin Book of Elizabethan Verse* (Harmondsworth, 1965), Patricia Thomson's *Elizabethan Lyrical Poets* (London, 1967) and Geoffrey Hiller's *Poems of the Elizabethan Age: An Anthology* (London, 1977). You can also look at the relevant sections of general anthologies like the *Oxford* and *New Oxford Books of English Verse* (1900, 1972), *The Albatross Book of Verse* (revised edn., London, 1960), the Penguin *Book of English Poetry* (enlarged edn., Harmondsworth, 1953) or even the first book of the classic Victorian collection, Palgrave's *The Golden Treasury* (1861).

Nearly all the Tudor 'poetic miscellanies' have been expertly edited by Hyder E. Rollins. There is also a fine edition of *England's Helicon* by Hugh Macdonald (London, 1949). Some representative poets have been usefully brought together in *Silver Poets of the Sixteenth Century*, ed. G. Bullett (London, 1947), *Silver Poets of the Seventeenth Century*, ed. G.A.E. Parfitt (London, 1974) and *Cavalier Poets*, ed. T. Clayton (Oxford, 1978); but the readings in the first book are not always reliable.

The Elizabethan sonnet-cycles were collected in two volumes by Sir Sidney Lee (London, 1904). There is also an excellent selection in *The Sonnet* ed. R.M. Bender and C.L. Squier (New York, 1965). The verses from the song-books have been collected in E.H. Fellowes's *English Madrigal Verse 1588–1632* (3rd edition, rev. F.W. Sternfeld & D. Greer, Oxford, 1967), and the epyllia or mythological tales in *Elizabethan Minor Epics*, ed. E.S. Donno (London, 1963) and *Elizabethan Narrative Verse*, ed. N. Alexander (London, 1967).

Renaissance poetry in other European languages is more accessible in English translation than before. H.H. Blanchard's *Prose and Poetry of the Continental Renaissance in Translation* (New York, 1949) is a comprehensive collection. F.J. Nichol's *An Anthology of Neo-Latin Poetry* (New Haven, 1979) is also very useful, and there is *Renaissance Latin Verse: An Anthology* edited by Alessandro Perosa and John Sparrow (London, 1980).

Turning to Italian poetry, Petrarch's love-poems are now fully available in an admirable translation by Robert M. Durling (*Petrarch's Lyric Poems*, Cambridge, Mass., 1976). The Elizabethan translations of Ariosto's *Orlando Furioso*, by Sir John Harington, and Tasso's *Jerusalem Delivered*, by Edward Fairfax, are in print; and there are recent translations of the former by Guido Waldman (Oxford, 1974) and Barbara Reynolds (Harmondsworth, 1975). Michelangelo's poems have been translated by Creighton Gilbert (1963). Other Italian Renaissance poetry can be found in *The Penguin Book of Italian Verse* (2nd edition, 1965). There is a good selection of French Renaissance poetry in vol. 2 of *The Penguin Book of French Verse* (1958), though (as with *Italian Verse*) the translations are fairly literal efforts confined to footnotes.

Renaissance continental poetry has been skilfully surveyed in *The Continental Renaissance 1500–1600*, ed. A.J. Krailsheimer (*Pelican Guides to European Literature*, Harmondsworth, 1971). Serviceable accounts of Elizabethan poetry may be found in all standard histories of English literature. The relevant volumes in some multi-volume series, like the *New Pelican Guide to English Literature*, the *Sphere History of English Literature*, and *Longman's History of English Literature*, are particularly useful. C.S. Lewis's longer volume in the Oxford History of English Literature, *English Literature in the Sixteenth Century Excluding Drama* (1954: recently reissued as *Poetry and Prose in the Sixteenth Century*), is full and lively if somewhat idiosyncratic. Douglas Bush's companion volume, *English Literature in the Earlier Seventeenth Century* (1962) is equally learned, and more equable in tone. Another valuable guide is Hallett Smith's *Elizabethan Poetry* (Cambridge, Mass., 1952).

The spirit of the 'new' English poetry may be gauged from two very different works: John Buxton's lucid and readable *Sir Philip Sidney and the English Renaissance* (London, 1954), and Richard Helgerson's later and more complex account in *Self-Crowned Laureates: Spenser, Jonson, Milton and the Literary System* (Berkeley, 1983). See also Yvor Winters's 'Poetic Styles, Old and New' in *Four Poets on Poetry*, ed. D.C. Allen (Baltimore, 1959) and 'Aspects of the Short Poem in the English Renaissance' in *Forms of Discovery* (Chicago, 1967); D.G. Rees's 'Italian and Italianate Poetry' in *Elizabethan Poetry* (Stratford-upon-Avon Studies 2, London, 1960); and G.K. Hunter's 'Drab and Golden Lyrics of the Renaissance' in *Forms of Lyric*, ed. R.A. Brower (New York, 1970).

A valuable counterweight is provided by A.C. Spearing's *Medieval to Renaissance in English Poetry* (Cambridge, 1985), especially the final chapter on Wyatt and Surrey; and by Philip Hobsbaum's essay on 'Elizabethan Poetry' in his *Tradition and Experiment in English Poetry* (London, 1979), even if Hobsbaum emphasizes the native and realistic elements of the poetry so much as to distort the total perspective. Of older studies, M.C. Bradbrook's *Shakespeare and Elizabethan Poetry* (London, 1951) exceeds the promise of its title to provide a general study of poetic forms and the milieu of the age.

Catherine Ing's *Elizabethan Lyrics* (London, 1951) gives a perceptive account of Elizabethan prosody, supplementing Enid Hamer's *The Metres of English Poetry* (London, 1930) and John Thompson's *The Founding of English Metre* (London, 1961). Language and diction have been studied in V.L. Rubel's *Poetic Diction in the English Renaissance* (New York, 1941) and A.C. Partridge's *Tudor to Augustan English* (London, 1969) and *The Language of Renaissance Poetry* (London, 1971).

On rhetoric, Brian Vickers's *Classical Rhetoric in English Poetry* (London, 1970) gives a simple account, and Rosemond Tuve's classic *Elizabethan and Metaphysical Imagery* (Chicago, 1947) a full and complex treatment touching upon some root principles of Elizabethan poetic language. W.J. Howell's *Logic and Rhetoric in England, 1500–1700* (Princeton, 1956) defines the background of Renaissance thought in this area. Elizabethan figures of speech are listed and explained in L.A. Sonnino, *A Handbook to Sixteenth-Century Rhetoric* (London, 1968).

The background to the poetry needs a reading list to itself. E.M.W. Tillyard's *The Elizabethan World Picture* (London, 1943) is still of use to beginners, though the very concept of a 'world-picture' has been discredited. Hardin Craig's *The Enchanted Glass* (New York, 1936) and Douglas Bush's *Prefaces to Renaissance Literature* go deeper into the thought of the age. Isobel Rivers's *Classical and*

Christian Ideas in English Renaissance Poetry (London, 1979) is a valuable introduction to many basic concepts.

A broader view of Renaissance life and culture is taken in *Background to the English Renaissance*, ed. J.B. Trapp (London, 1974). *Shakespeare's England* (2 vols., 1904) is still a treasure-house of information on Elizabethan life; so is Vol. I of the more recent *William Shakespeare: His World, His Work, His Influence*, ed. J.F. Andrews (New York, 1985). John Buxton's *Elizabethan Taste* provides a reliable guide to the art and culture of the age. A.L. Rowse's *The Elizabethan Renaissance* (2 vols., London, 1972) is informative and readable if sometimes a little sensational.

An important aspect of Renaissance culture in relation to Renaissance poetry is traced by H.A. Mason in *Humanism and Poetry in the Early Tudor Period* (London, 1959), and another by Daniel Javitch in *Poetry and Courtliness in Renaissance England* (Princeton, 1978). Commencing his study at a slightly later date, David Norbrook in *Politics and Poetry in the English Renaissance* (London, 1984) traces the intimate connexion between the poetry and the life of the times.

The rediscovery of the classics, and their impact on Renaissance poetry, is treated simply yet exhaustively in Gilbert Highet's *The Classical Tradition* (Oxford, 1949), while T.W. Baldwin's *William Shakespere's Small Latine and Lesse Greek* (2 vols., Urbana, 1944) affords a mine of information for the advanced student. On the use of classical mythology, Douglas Bush's *Mythology and the Renaissance Tradition in English Poetry* (Minneapolis, 1933) has become a classic.

Critical ideas are surveyed in J.E. Spingarn's *A History of Literary Criticism in the Renaissance* (2nd edition, New York, 1908); J.W.H. Atkins's *English Literary Criticism: The Renaissance* (London, 1947); and all too briefly in the relevant section of W.K. Wimsatt and C. Brooks's *Literary Criticism: A Short History* (New York, 1957). A handy selection of the actual critical writings can be found in O.B. Hardison's *English Literary Criticism: The Renaissance* (New York, 1963). A fuller collection is available between G. Gregory Smith's *Elizabethan Critical Essays* (2 vols., Oxford, 1904) and J.E. Spingarn's *Critical Essays of the Seventeenth Century*, vol. 1 (Oxford, 1908). The serious student should take special heed of Sir Philip Sidney's *An Apology for Poetry* (also called *The Defence of Poesie*), preferably in Geoffrey Shepherd's admirable edition (London, 1965). He should also pay some attention to Puttenham's *The Art of English Poesy* (to be found in Gregory Smith's collection).

Sadly, most major continental critical works of this period have not been translated into English. Exceptions are Cintho Giraldi's discourse *On Romances* (trans. H.L. Snuggs, Lexington, 1968); Torquato Tasso's *Discourses on the Heroic Poem* (trans. M. Cavalchini & I. Samuel, Oxford, 1973); and extracts from J.C. Scaliger's *Seven Books of Poetics* in F.D. Padelford's *Scaliger on Poetry* (Illinois, 1905). There is also an indispensable body of extracts from major critics and theorists in *Literary Criticism: Plato to Dryden* ed. A.H. Gilbert (New York, 1940).

The crucial matter of poetic types or genres has been studied by Alastair Fowler in *Kinds of Literature* (Oxford, 1982). J.A.K. Thomson's simple historical account (*Classical Influences on English Poetry*, London, 1951), remains permanently useful. Neither book, however, deals exclusively with the Renaissance.

The actual criticism of the poetry is so vast that I can list only the briefest selection. Perhaps it is just as well that the student should not let too many critics come between him and the poetry. There are many serviceable anthologies of critical essays, among them *Elizabethan Poetry* (Stratford-upon-Avon Studies 2, London, 1960) and *Elizabethan Poetry: Modern Essays in Criticism*, ed. Paul J. Alpers (New York, 1968). There are also collections of essays on major poets in series like *The Critical Heritage* and *Twentieth Century Views*.

The development of the Elizabethan lyric is traced by Jerome Mazzaro in *Transformations in the English Renaissance Lyric* (Ithaca, 1970). Mazzaro has necessarily to pay much attention to the musical element, which is the sole subject of Brian Pattison's *Music and Poetry of the English Renaissance* (London, 1948), John Stevens's *Music and Poetry in the Early Tudor Court* (London, 1961) and Winifred Maynard's more exhaustive *Elizabethan Lyric Poetry and Its Music* (Oxford, 1986). Harold Toliver's *Lyric Provinces in the English Renaissance* (Columbus, Ohio, 1985) offers deep if somewhat abstruse insight into many lyric poets.

On Elizabethan pastoral, see W.W. Greg's *Pastoral Poetry and Pastoral Drama* (London, 1906), Helen Cooper's *Pastoral: Medieval into Renaissance* (Ipswich, 1977), and Sukanta Chaudhuri's *Renaissance Pastoral and Its English Developments* (Oxford, 1989); and on the epyllion, William Keach's *Elizabethan Erotic Narratives* (New Brunswick, 1977).

On love-poetry and the sonnet, the standard handbook is still J.W. Lever's *The Elizabethan Love-Sonnet* (London, 1956). A wider perspective is afforded by J.B. Broadbent's *Poetic Love* (London, 1964) and A.J. Smith's *The Metaphysics of Love* (Cambridge, 1985). Petrachism in particular is the subject of Leonard Foster's study *The Icy Fire* (Cambridge, 1969).

The leading poets are obviously discussed in the works listed above, but they need separate treatment as well. The standard edition of Wyatt is by J. van Daalder (Oxford, 1975). R.A. Rebholz's edition (Harmondsworth, 1978) is fully, almost overmuch, annotated. The earlier edition by Kenneth Muir and Patricia Thomson (Liverpool, 1969) was involved in textual controversy. On Wyatt, see Patricia Thomson's *Sir Thomas Wyatt and His Background* (London, 1964). Emrys Jones has edited Surrey's *Poems* (Oxford, 1964).

The standard text of Spenser's *Poetical Works* is edited by J.C. Smith and E. de Selincourt (Oxford, 1912). The Variorum Edition of the Works, ed. E. Greenlaw, C.G. Osgood and F.M. Padelford (Baltimore, 1932–49) is a monumental work with elaborate notes and other apparatus. The most useful editions of *The Faerie Queene* for students are by T.S. Roche (Harmondsworth, 1978), A.C. Hamilton (London, 1977) and, for Books I and II, P.C. Bayley (Oxford, 1965, 1966).

Books on Spenser are legion. P.C. Bayley's *Edmund Spenser, Prince of Poets* (London, 1971) provides a simple, reliable introduction, and Helena Shire's *A Preface to Spenser* (London, 1978) a somewhat esoteric one. W.L. Renwick's *Edmund Spenser: An Essay on Renaissance Poetry* (London, 1925) is an old-fashioned but valuable and immensely sensitive study of Spenser's art. On *The Faerie Queene* in particular, good introductions are available in Leicester Bradner's *Edmund Spenser and the Faerie Queene* (Chicago, 1948), Graham Hough's *A Preface to The Faerie Queene* (London, 1962), Rosemary Freeman's *The Faerie Queene: A Companion for Readers* (London, 1970) and Humphrey Tonkin's *The Faerie Queene* (London, 1989). H.S.V. Jones's *A Spenser Handbook* (New York, 1930) is a useful guide. More advanced studies lie beyond the scope of this book. I shall mention only three classic works: M.P. Parker's *The Allegory of The Faerie Queene* (Oxford, 1960), J.E. Hankins's *Source and Meaning in Spenser's Allegory* (Oxford, 1971) and James Nohrnberg's monumental *The Analogy of The Faerie Queene* (Oxford, 1976).

Marlowe's *Poems*, including *Hero and Leander*, have been edited by Millar Maclure (Manchester, 1968) and by Stephen Orgel in the Penguin *Complete Poems and Translations* (Harmondsworth, 1971). The standard edition of Shakespeare's Poems (excluding the sonnets) is by F.T. Prince in the New Arden series (London, 1960). W. G. Ingram and T. Redpath have produced an excellent student's edition of Shakespeare's Sonnets (London, 1964) and John Dover Wilson the leading scholarly one, if a little eccentric at times (Cambridge, 1966). A.L. Rowse's edition (London, 1964) has a useful explanatory paraphrase.

There are innumerable critical studies of Shakespeare's Sonnets. But any selection must include G. Wilson Knight's profound if somewhat mystical *The Mutual Flame* (London, 1955); J.B. Leishman's *Themes and Variations in Shakespeare's Sonnets* (London, 1961); Paul Turner's *Shakespeare and the Nature of Time* (Oxford, 1971); Anne Ferry's *All in War with Time* (Cambridge, Mass., 1975), which also treats Donne, Jonson and Marvell; G.F. Waller's *The Strong Necessity of Time* (The Hague, 1976); and the works mentioned above by Lever, Broadbent and Smith.

Sidney's *Poems* have been elaborately edited by W. Ringler Jr. (Oxford, 1962). Dorothy O'Connell's *Sir Philip Sidney* (Oxford, 1977) and A.C. Hamilton's *Sir Philip Sidney: A Study of His Life and Works* (Cambridge, 1977) provide excellent introductions. Daniel's *Poems and A Defence of Ryme* have been handily edited (though without explanatory notes) by A.C. Sprague (Cambridge, Mass., 1930).

J.W. Hebel, supported by Kathleen Tillotson, produced the massive Tercentenary edition of Drayton's *Works* (5 vols., Oxford, 1931–41). John Buxton's 2-volume selection (London, 1953) is handier for the student. Drayton has not received the critical attention he deserves; but Richard Hardin's *Michael Drayton and the Passing of Elizabethan England* (Laurence, Kansas, 1973) is a valuable study. The standard account of Drayton and his associates is in Joan Grundy's *The Spenserian Poets* (London, 1969).

The monumental edition of Ben Jonson's *Works* by C.H. Herford and P. & E. Simpson (11 vols., Oxford, 1925–52) includes his poems (vol. 8) with commentary (vol. 11). There is a well-annotated edition by George Parfitt (Penguin English Poets, Harmondsworth, 1975), another by Ian Donaldson (Oxford, 1975), and a useful critical account in J.G. Nichols's *The Poetry of Ben Jonson* (London, 1969). Ben

Jonson figures largely in F.R. Leavis's classic essay 'The Line of Wit' in *Revaluation* (London, 1936). Something of its spirit is recalled by John Hollander's brilliant 'Ben Jonson and the Modality of Verse' (*Vision and Resonance*, Oxford, 1975).

These essays also touch upon Metaphysical poetry. The Metaphysicals are being reserved for a separate volume in this series. But obviously, the links between Metaphysical and other English Renaissance poetry, especially earlier seventeenth-century poetry, cannot be overlooked. They emerge from any standard anthology like H.J.C. Grierson's *Metaphysical Lyrics and Poems* (Oxford, 1921) or Helen Gardner's *The Metaphysical Poets* (Harmondsworth, 1957); or perhaps even better from the once popular *A Treasury of Seventeenth Century English Verse* edited by H.J. Massingham (London, 1919). The links between Metaphysical and other English poetry have been investigated, and perhaps even overplayed, by Rosemond Tuve (see above). The links with European poetry generally have been studied by J. Cohen in *The Baroque Lyric* (London, 1963).

44 *Henry Howard, Earl of Surrey*

2 *no thing* obviously pronounced as two words
3 *air* i.e., wind
4 *chair* chariot, Petrarch has *stellato carro*, 'starry' or 'star-studded car'.
5 *work* toss, move violently (OED 34)
6 *wring* rack, oppress
8–9 Typically Petrarchan paradoxes
9 *doubtful* fearful: an oxymoron with *ease*
10 *sometime* sometimes, now and then
11 *disease* Perhaps *dis-ease*, distress or disquiet; but in Petrarchan convention, love could actually be seen as an illness to be cured from the very source (i.e., the mistress) that had caused it: see l.14.
12 *pang* pain
sting hurt, pierce
14 *should rid* i.e., that should rid

Sir Thomas Wyatt

1 Sonnet: 'The long love'

[Closely follows Petrarch's *Rime* 140, also translated by Surrey. This poem exploits the common Petrarchan paradox of applying war-imagery to love—but in a vein very different from the battle of the sexes, implying rather a moral battle in idealized vein. The mistress is loved because she will not admit love: the lover's desire is necessarily frustrated by the very virtue that arouses it. Contrast Wyatt's other sonnets in bitter or ironical vein. See also Introduction, pp. 9–11.]

The long love that in my thought doth harbour
And in mine heart doth keep his residence,
Into my face presseth with bold pretence,
And therein campeth, spreading his banner.
She that me learneth to love and suffer
And will that my trust and lust's negligence
Be reined by reason, shame and reverence,
With his hardiness taketh displeasure.
Wherewithal unto the heart's forest he fleeth,
Leaving his enterprise with pain and cry,
And there him hideth, and not appeareth.
What may I do, when my master feareth,
But in the field with him to live and die?
For good is the life ending faithfully.

1 *long* long-standing (OED 11) *thought* mind
harbour lodge, encamp (often with notion of hiding: OED 7)
3 *presseth* charges, rushes; but also 'expresses' (itself)
pretence parade, display (OED 2)
4 *spreading his banner* i.e., offering battle
5 *learneth* teaches *suffer* be patient

6 *will* will have, wishes (with *she* as subject). Some mss. have *wills* *trust* confidence, boldness
lust desire, longing (no bad sense: OED 2)
negligence 'careless confidence' (Padelford); recklessness
7 *reined* bridled, checked; with pun on *reigned*, ruled
8 *hardiness* boldness, audacity
9 *wherewithal* wherewith, at which
heart's forest Inaugurates the common pun on *heart/hart*, applying the metaphor of stag-hunting to love. Buxton suggests that *harbour* (l.1) is the hunter's term for a stag's retreat. But retreating soldiers might also shelter in a forest.
12 *my master* i.e., Love, now clearly Cupid or the love-god (as from the start in Petrarch). He is seen as a feudal lord, and the poet as a soldier in his retinue. But the poet is also in service to his mistress, Love's adversary. This conflict or paradox underlies the poem.

2 Sonnet: 'Each man me telleth'

[Overthrows the ideal of constancy. Pragmatic proposal of mutual faith or none: perhaps in love, but in the context of the poem, *applying* the concept of unfaithfulness in love to shifting worldly or political relationships.]

Each man me telleth I change most my device;
And on my faith, me think it good reason
To change propose like after the season,
For in every case to keep still one guise
Is meet for them that would be taken wise:
And I am not of such manner condition,
But treated after a diverse fashion,
and thereupon my diverseness doth rise.
But you that blame this diverseness most,
Change you no more, but still after one rate
Treat ye me well, and keep ye in the same state:
And while with me doth dwell this wearied ghost
My word nor I shall not be variable,
But always one, your own both firm and stable.

1 *device* (a) purpose (b) strategy, tactics (c) coat-of-arms or insignia (which implies political allegiance)

2 *me think* It seems to me: old impersonal construction

3 *propose* purpose *like after* according to *season* time, occasion

4 *case* situation

5 *meet* fitting *taken wise* thought (falsely) to be wise

6 *of such manner condition* of such a sort (*condition*, either 'character, disposition' or 'state, situation' — the latter implying that his worldly situation being unstable, he is forced to change accordingly)

7 *diverse* (a) different (b) variable (which accords better with line 8)

9 *blame* censure, criticize

10 *still* always *after one rate* at the same pace; steadily, sustainedly

11 *ye* plural: presumably addressed to his hostile fellow-courtiers, but perhaps the honorific plural for his beloved

12 'While my soul remains with me', i.e., until my death
wearied exhausted, worn-out (by frustrated love)
ghost spirit, soul

13 A double negative, permissible in Wyatt's day

3 Sonnet: 'Farewell, Love'

[Most characteristic of Wyatt's 'un-Petrarchan' ironic or pragmatic vein. The spiritual note is tempered by a very human frustration and exasperation.]

Farewell, Love, and all thy laws for ever!
Thy baited hooks shall tangle me no more:
Senec and Plato call me from thy lore,
To perfect wealth my wit for to endeavour.
In blind error when I did persever,
Thy sharp repulse, that pricketh aye so sore,
Hath taught me to set in trifles no store,
And 'scape forth, since liberty is liever.
Therefore farewell: go trouble younger hearts,

And in me claim no more authority;
With idle youth go use thy property,
And thereon spend thy many brittle darts:
For hitherto though I have lost all my time,
Me lusteth no longer rotten boughs to climb.

1 *Love* Clearly the god of love or Cupid (cf.1.12n). Love and Law are traditionally opposed. It is ironical to see one as subject to the other.

2 *baited hooks* a fishing image

3 *Senec* Seneca, the Roman Stoic philosopher
Plato who views the spirit or idea (rather than matter, which can imply fleshly lust) as the prime reality
lore learning

4 *perfect wealth* i.e., wisdom or spirituality
wit intelligence, faculties *endeavour* exert, exercise (OED 1b)

5 *blind* as Cupid was said to be
persever clearly to be pronounced 'per-*se*-ver'

6 *repulse* Presumably by the mistress. The rejection of love may thus be caused by disappointment rather than true spirituality. The 'baited hooks' that attract have now become a goad that drives away. *aye* always

8 *liever* preferable

9 *younger hearts* Suggests another reason for the farewell to love: old age.

11 *idle* frivolous, foolish (OED 2)

12 *property* characteristic, power
brittle perishable, ephemeral (OED 1b) *darts* arrows. Cupid's golden arrows caused love, the leaden hate.

14 *Me lusteth* I desire: old impersonal construction
rotten boughs Proverbial: 'Who trusts to rotten boughs may fall.'

4 Sonnet: 'My galley charged'

[Translates Petrarch's famous poem, *Rime* 189. The image of the sorrowful lover as a distressed or shipwrecked mariner goes back to Horace, *Odes* I.v.]

My galley charged with forgetfulness
Thorough sharp seas in winter nights doth pass
'Tween rock and rock, and eke mine enemy alas,
That is my lord, steereth with cruelness,
And every oar a thought in readiness,
As though that death were light in such a case.
And endless wind doth tear the sail apace,
Of forced sighs and trusty fearfulness;
A rain of tears, a cloud of dark disdain
Hath done the wearied cords great hinderance,
Wreathed with error, and eke with ignorance.
The stars be hid that led me to this pain,
Drowned is reason that should me comfort,
And I remain despairing of the port.

1 *galley* Used precisely: the old Mediterranean galley had both sails and oars, as here. Petrarch has only *la nave*, 'ship'.
charged laden; hence oppressed or afflicted (OED 11)
forgetfulness either the lover's, of everything other than love; or the mistress's, towards the lover

2 *sharp* violent, turbulent (OED 4d)

3 *rock and rock* Petrarch has 'Scylla and Charybdis', the proverbial rock and whirlpool. *eke* also, further—i.e., more alarmingly still

3–4 *mine enemy . . . my lord* i.e., Love. Petrarch has 'My lord, or rather still more (*anzi*) my enemy'.

5 *in readiness* swift, easily aroused

6 i.e., scorning all fear of death

7 *tear* pull or blow off the mast (OED 5)

8 Refers to *wind* (l.7) *forced* perhaps 'forceful, violent'
trusty fearfulness perhaps 'mingled hopes and fears'
trusty 'trustful, confident' (OED 1, quoting Wyatt), hence possibly 'hopeful'

10 *wearied* strained, worn-out *cords* sail-ropes
hinderance damage

11 *wreathed* woven or twisted, as cord-strands are

12 *The stars* the mistress's eyes: a standard Petrarchan conceit

13 *comfort* support, strengthen (L. *fortis*, strong). Should perhaps read *consort*, 'accompany, keep together', said especially of ships (OED 5b)

14 *of the port* i.e., of reaching the port

5 : 'Resound my voice, ye woods'

[Works the Petrarchan vein of the sorrowful lover's recourse to nature. (See Petrarch, *Rime* 35, 67, 129, 176, 237.) This interaction between nature and man, and ascription of human feelings to nature, is a notable innovation of Petrarchan poetry.

The poem is in rime royal.]

Resound my voice, ye woods that hear me plain,
Both hills and vales causing reflection;
And rivers eke record ye of my pain,
Which hath ye oft forc'd by compassion
As judges to hear mine exclamation,
Among whom pity I find doth remain:
Where I it seek alas there is disdain.

Oft ye rivers, to hear my woeful sound
Have stopp'd your course; and plainly to express
Many a tear, by moisture of the ground
The earth hath wept, to hear my heaviness,
Which causeless to suffer without redress
The hugy oaks have roared in the wind,
Each thing, me thought, complaining in their kind.

Why then alas doth not she on me rue?
Or is her heart so hard that no pity
May in it sink, my joy for to renew?
O stony heart! how hath this joined thee,
So cruel that art, cloaked with beauty?
No grace to me from thee there may proceed,
But, as rewarded, death for to be my meed.

1 *resound* echo *plain* complain
2 *reflection* echo

3 *eke* also *record* (a) memorize, remember (OED 1,4); (b) relate (OED 8), presumably by the river's murmur (c) bear witness (OED 10) — hence *judges* (1.5).

4–5 *compassion, exclamation* Then pronounced *commpass-i-on, exclamat-i-on.*

9 *plainly to express* to express its feelings plainly; but *express* also = press out, exude

10 *moisture of the ground* the dew or earth's 'tears'

11 *heaviness* burden of grief

12 Syntax unclear. Perhaps the whole line is the object of *roared* — (1.13), used transitively: the oaks have 'roared' or declared loudly that it is the lover's heavy grief to suffer causelessly.

13 *hugy* variant of *huge*, fifteenth to seventeenth century

14 *complaining* lamenting
in their kind after their nature, in their own way

15 *rue* take pity

16–18 Syntax uncertain, but clearly means 'How have these opposites, of cruelty and beauty, come to be joined in the same person?'

19 *cloaked* disguised

20 *grace* favour, pity; stock use in love poetry of a basically theological term

21 *as rewarded* as though I were being fitly rewarded
meed reward, recompense

Henry Howard, Earl of Surrey

6 Sonnet: 'The soot season'

[Adapted from Petrarch's *Rime* 310, among the sonnets written after the death of his beloved Laura. In Surrey, the cause of the lover's sorrow is not clearly stated, and the description of nature takes up nearly the whole poem. The language is 'a tissue of traditional phrasing drawn from English medieval poetry' (Emrys Jones).

Note the rhyme-scheme: virtually inaugurating the 'English' sonnet form and even exceeding it by having only two rhymes.]

The soot season, that bud and bloom forth brings,
With green hath clad the hill and eke the vale.
The nightingale with feathers new she sings,
The turtle to her make hath told her tale.
Summer is come, for every spray now springs;
The hart hath hung his old head on the pale;
The buck in brake his winter coat he flings;
The fishes float with new repaired scale;
The adder all her slough away she slings;
Th swift swallow pursueth the flies smale;
The busy bee her honey now she mings.
Winter is worn, that was the flowers' bale.
    And thus I see among these pleasant things
    Each care decays, and yet my sorrow springs.

1 *soot* variant of *sweet*
2 *eke* also
4 *turtle* turtle-dove
make mate, partner *told her tale* said what she had to, repeated her message (of love)
5 *spray* shoot, small plant *springs* grows (OED 8); but also perhaps 'leaps up', in swift and vigorous growth

6 *hart* specifically the male red deer (cf. *buck*, 1.7)
hung . . . pale 'hung up his old antlers on a stake or post': a fanciful way of alluding to the hart's growing new antlers every year

7 *buck* the male fallow deer *in brake* among the bushes
winter coat such as animals grow in many cold countries
flings i.e., throws away, discards: again said fancifully

8 *float* swim (old use, of fishes: OED 3)
repaired restored, refurbished

9 *slings* throws away (OED 2)

10 *smale* small: a common early variant deriving from Old English

11 *her honey . . . mings* remembers her (task of gathering or attending to) honey

12 *worn* exhausted, finished *bale* evil, torment

13 *pleasant* in a strong sense: delightful, joyful

7 Sonnet: 'Alas, so all things now'

[Freely adapted from Petrarch's *Rime* 164.]

Alas, so all things now do hold their peace,
Heaven and earth disturbed in no thing:
The beasts, the air, the birds their song do cease;
The night's chair the stars about doth bring.
Calm is the sea, the waves work less and less;
So am not I, whom love alas doth wring,
Bringing before my face the great increase
Of my desires, whereat I weep and sing
In joy and woe as in a doubtful ease.
For my sweet thoughts sometime do pleasure bring,
But by and by the cause of my disease
Gives me a pang that inwardly doth sting.
  When that I think what grief it is again
  To live and lack the thing should rid my pain.

1 *so* apparently a vague intensive

2 *no thing* obviously pronounced as two words
3 *air* i.e., wind
4 *chair* chariot, Petrarch has *stellato carro*, 'starry' or 'star-studded car'.
5 *work* toss, move violently (OED 34)
6 *wring* rack, oppress
8–9 Typically Petrarchan paradoxes
9 *doubtful* fearful: an oxymoron with *ease*
10 *sometime* sometimes, now and then
11 *disease* Perhaps *dis-ease*, distress or disquiet; but in Petrarchan convention, love could actually be seen as an illness to be cured from the very source (i.e., the mistress) that had caused it: see l.14.
12 *pang* pain
sting hurt, pierce
14 *should rid* i.e., that should rid

George Turberville

8 : To His Friend

[This lyric appeared in 1587, after *The Shepherd's Calendar* but before the real spate of love–sonnets and lyrics. It thus sustains the vein struck by Turberville in 1567 in *Epitaphs, Epigrams, Songs and Sonnets*—lyrics preceding the great flowering of the 'new poetry' but notably anticipating it.]

I wot full well that beauty cannot last:
No rose that springs but lightly doth decay,
And feature like a lily leaf doth waste
Or as the cowslip in the month of May.
I know that tract of time doth conquer all,
And beauty's buds like fading flowers do fall.

That famous dame, fair Helen, lost her hue
When wither'd age with wrinkles chang'd her cheeks.
Her lovely looks did loathsomeness ensue,
That was the *A per se* of all the Greeks.
And sundry mo that were as fair as she,
Yet Helen was as fresh as fresh might be.

No force for that, I price your beauty light
If so I find you steadfast in good will.
Though few there are that do in age delight,
I was your friend, and so do purpose still;
No change of looks shall breed my change of love,
Nor beauty's want my first good will remove.

1 *wot* know
2 *lightly* swiftly (OED 5)
3 *feature* features, face (OED 3), hence beauty

waste wear away, decay

5 *tract* passing, motion

6 Note the playing off of *buds* against *fading flowers*

7 *dame* lady

hue colour, complexion

9 'Her beauty was followed by, or turned into, ugliness.'

ensue follow, succeed

10 *A per se* (Latin) 'A by itself', the letter A—hence the first, chief or best

11 *And sundry mo* An old construction: 'Even though there were many others' *mo* more

12 *as fresh . . . be* i.e., the most beautiful

13 *No . . . that* It does not matter

price value

14 *If so* 'If it be that', if

16 *so do purpose* wish to be such

still always

17 *breed* generate, cause

18 *want* lack

Sir Thomas Sackville

9 : From *A Mirror For Magistrates*

[Between 1355 and 1374, Giovanni Boccaccio of Italy inaugurated an influential line of poetry with his *De Casibus Virorum Illustrium* ('The Falls of Famous Men'). It recounted many cases of downfall and death from positions of wealth, fame and power. The aim was not only to point a general moral but in particular to provide a 'mirror for magistrates', a looking-glass where all rulers might see their precarious situation and uncertain end. The Monk's Tale in Chaucer's *Canterbury Tales* provides an early English instance of the genre.

De Casibus was partly rendered into English by John Lydgate in the fifteenth century as *The Falls of Princes. A Mirror for Magistrates* testifies to the popularity of this late-medieval genre in England at the very time the 'new' poetry was being born. (See Introduction p. 8).

The *Mirror* is a work of many hands. The most important are William Baldwin (the compiler and moving spirit), George Ferrers, Thomas Chaloner, Thomas Churchyard, Francis Segar and of course Sackville. First published in 1559, the collection was expanded in subsequent editions. Sackville's pieces, an 'Induction' and the 'Complaint of Buckingham', were added in 1563.

Henry Stafford, Duke of Buckingham was Richard III's chief aide and counsellor in the latter's ruthless rise to power. But the two ultimately fell out through mutual distrust, and Buckingham led an unsuccessful rebellion. Fleeing after this failure, he took shelter with one Humphrey (or Ralph) Bannister, whom he had greatly benefited but who now betrayed him. In the *Mirror,* Buckingham (who had been recounting his life to the narrator during the latter's visit to hell) swoons at this point of his narrative. Then follows the passage printed here.]

Midnight was come, and every vital thing
With sweet sound sleep their weary limbs did rest.
The beasts were still, the little birds that sing
Now sweetly slept besides their mother's breast:
The old and all were shrouded in their nest.
    The waters calm, the cruel seas did cease:
    The woods, the fields, and all things held their peace.

The golden stars were whirl'd amid their race
And on the earth did laugh with twinkling light
When each thing, nestled in his resting place,
Forgat day's pain with pleasure of the night.
The hare had not the greedy hounds in sight,
    The fearful deer of death stood not in doubt,
    The partridge drept not of the falcon's foot.

The ugly bear now minded not the stake,
Nor how the cruel mastiffs do him tear.
The stag lay still unroused from the brake,
The foamy boar fear'd not the hunter's spear.
All thing was still in desert, bush and brere:
    With quiet heart now from their travails' rest,
    Soundly they slept in midst of all their rest.

When Buckingham, amid his plaint oppresst,
With surging sorrows and with pinching pains
In sort thus sown'd, and with a sigh he ceas'd
To tellen forth the treachery and the trains
Of Bannister, which him so sore distrains
    That from a sigh he falls into a sound,
    And from a sound lieth raging on the ground.

. . . . .

Dead lay his corpse, as dead as any stone,
Till swelling sighs storming within his breast
Uprais'd his head, that downward fell anon,
With looks upcast and sighs that never ceas'd.
Forth stream'd the tears, records of his unrest,

When he with shrieks thus grovelling on the ground,
Y-bray'd these words with shrill and doleful sound.

'Heaven and earth, and ye eternal lamps
That, in the heavens wrapt, will us to rest,
Thou bright Phoebe, that clearest the night's damps,
Witness the plaints that, in these pangs opprest,
I, woeful wretch, unlade out of my breast,
And let me yield my last words ere I part.
You, you I call to record of my smart.'

[There follows a long cursing tirade against Bannister.]

This said, he flung his retchless arms abroad,
And grovelling flat upon the ground he lay,
Which with his teeth he all to gnash'd and gnaw'd;
Deep groans he fet, as he that would away:
But lo, in vain he did the death assay,
Although I think was never man that knew
Such deadly pains where death did not ensue.

So strove he thus a while as with the death,
Now pale as lead, and cold as any stone;
Now still as calm, now storming forth a breath
Of smoky sighs, as breath and all were gone.
But every thing hath end: so he anon
Came to himself, when with a sigh outbray'd,
With woeful cheer these woeful words he said:

'Ah, where am I? What thing, or whence, is this?
Who reft my wits? or how do I thus lie?
My limbs do quake, my thought aghasted is.
Why sigh I so? Or whereunto do I
Thus grovel on the ground?' And by and by
Uprais'd he stood, and with a sigh hath stay'd,
When to himself returned, thus he said:

'Sufficeth now this plaint and this regret
Whereof my heart his bottom hath unfraught;
And of my death let peers and princes weet
The world's untrust, that they thereby be taught,
And in her wealth, sith that such change is wrought,
    Hope not too much, but in the midst of all
    Think on my death, and what may them befall.

So long as Fortune would permit the same,
I liv'd in rule and riches with the best,
And pass'd my time in honour and in fame,
That of mishap no fear was in my breast.
But false Fortune, when I suspected least,
    Did turn the wheel, and with a doleful fall
    Hath me bereft of honour, life, and all.

Lo, what avails in riches' floods that flows,
Though she so smil'd as all the world were his?
Even kings and kesars biden Fortune's throws,
And simple sort must bear it as it is.
Take heed by me, that blith'd in baleful bliss:
    My rule, my riches, royal blood and all,
    When Fortune frown'd, the feller made my fall.'

1 *vital* living (Latin *vita*, life)
5 *shrouded* sheltered (OED 2)
6 *the . . . cease* The turbulent seas were still
8 *amid their race* in their course
11 *forgat* forgot: the old past tense
12-18 *hare, deer . . . boar* the constellations of these names as well as the animals
13 *doubt* fear
14 *drept* Hard to explain. Perhaps the past tense of *dreep*, 'to faint, to languish'; or of *drepe*, 'to strike, to kill': but neither seems to have been used with *of* in this way. Conceivably a mistake for *drempte*, 'dreamt'. *foot* i.e., talons
15 *minded* thought of, worried about (OED 8)

stake to which it would be tied and attacked by mastiffs (l.16) in the cruel sport of bear-baiting

17 *unroused* i.e., by hunters *brake* bush, cover

18 *foamy* i.e., frothing at the mouth

19 *brere* brier, thorn-bush(es). Here clearly pronounced 'breer', as formerly, hence the spelling *brere* retained.

20 'With a heart now quiet after their travails'

21 *their rest* the rest of their kind, their fellows

23 *pinching* distressing, oppressive (OED 7)

24 *in sort* in this way *sowned* swooned

25 *trains* schemes, wiles (OED *train* sb.2)

26 *distrains* distresses, oppresses

27 *sound* 'swound', swoon

29 *corpse* body (Latin *corpus*): he is not really dead

31 *anon* soon, presently

35 *y-bray'd* cried out, 'uttered harshly' (OED 1)

36 *eternal lamps* i.e., stars

37 *wrapt* In the old Ptolemaic astronomy, the stars and planets were set in concentric spheres, each 'wrapped' or enclosed by the next. *will us to rest* desire or determine that we should sleep (by their rising at nightfall)

38 *Phoebe* Diana, the moon-goddess *damps* fogs, mists

39 *pangs* pains

40 *unlade* unload, unburden

42 *smart* pain; hence, sorrow

43 *retchless* reckless; distracted, uncontrolled
abroad broadly, widely

45 *all to* An emphatic adverbial phrase: soundly (OED *all* a.15), forcibly

46 *fet* drew forth, brought out (related to *fetch*) *away* as verb: depart, die

47 *did the death assay* sought to die (This would have meant release: as a soul in hell, he was doomed to endless suffering.)

51 *pale* i.e., grey or ashen

52 *still as calm* either 'as still as calm', 'as still as still can be'; or 'as still as a calm at sea' (contrast *storming*)

53 'As though he were drawing his last breath'

54 *anon* see l.31n

55 *outbray'd* cf. *y-bray'd*, l.35.

56 *cheer* look, countenance

59 *aghasted* terrified, amazed

62 *stay'd* stopped, ceased to speak

64 *regret* complaint, lament (OED 1)

65 *his bottom hath unfraught* unloaded or unburdened its deepest sorrow (*his*, the old possessive of *it*)

66 *of* out of, (as a lesson) from *peers* noblemen
weet know, learn

67 *untrust* treachery—hence fickleness, and perhaps transience

68 *her* i.e., the world's, worldly *sith* since, seeing that

69 *midst* The original has the old variant *myds*

71 *Fortune* Conceived from Roman times as a goddess: the blind arbiter of change in human life, hence the governing force behind the 'falls of princes' and 'tragedy' in the medieval sense, which survived into the Renaissance.

76 *the wheel* the traditional attribute of Fortune. Its turns brought about changes of human state.

78 'What does it profit them who flow in floods of riches?'

79 *she* i.e., Fortune *as* as though

80 *kesars* 'Caesars' or 'kaisars', emperors. *Kings and kesars* was a stock alliterative phrase.
biden abide by, submit to. The *-en* is a plural ending.
throws overthrows, with a hint of throws at dice

81 *simple sort* the common people

82 *blith'd* was blithe or merry *baleful* evil, harmful

84 *feller* more cruel or painful

Edmund Spenser

10 : *The Shepherd's Calendar*, 'June'

[Spenser virtually inaugurated English Renaissance pastoral with *The Shepherd's Calendar* in 1579. As the title suggests, it contains twelve eclogues for the twelve months. Their narrative continuity has sometimes been over-stressed, as also their allusions to topical matters, or the connexion between the eclogues and the months to which they refer. But the pieces are certainly interrelated, presenting a consistent shepherd world whose characters and situations recur from poem to poem. Most sustainedly, the whole sequence reflects the story of the shepherd-poet Colin Clout's unrequited love for Rosalind. Colin seems to be a persona of Spenser himself; he recurs as such in the later poems *Colin Clout's Come Home Again* and *The Faerie Queene* Book VI.

In this poem, set in a summer's day in June, Hobbinoll is probably Spenser's friend, the scholar and critic Gabriel Harvey. The contrast between the happy settled shepherd and the unhappy wandering one goes back to Virgil's Eclogue I (where the happy shepherd seems to stand for the poet himself) and its medieval redaction, Petrarch's Eclogue I (where the sides have changed, and the poet is identified with the unhappy wanderer, as in Spenser).

A mysterious 'E.K.' added copious notes to the text. A few of these are cited below.]

Hobbinoll

Lo, Colin, here the place whose pleasant site
From other shades hath wean'd my wand'ring mind.
Tell me, what wants me here to work delight?
The simple air, the gentle warbling wind,
So calm, so cool, as nowhere else I find;
The grassy ground with dainty daisies dight;

The bramble bush, where birds of every kind
To the water's fall their tunes attemper right.

Colin

O happy Hobbinoll, I bless thy state!
Thou Paradise hast found, which Adam lost.
Here wander may thy flocks early or late
Withouten dread of wolves to bene y-tost.
Thy lovely lays here may'st thou freely boast.
But I, unhappy man, whom cruel fate
And angry gods pursue from coast to coast,
Can nowhere find to shroud my luckless pate.

Hobbinoll

Then if by me thou list advised be,
Forsake the soil that so doth thee bewitch.
Leave me these hills where harbrough nis to see,
Nor holly bush, nor brere, nor winding witch,
And to the dales resort, where shepherds rich
And fruitful flocks bene everywhere to see.
Here no night-ravens lodge more black than pitch,
Nor elvish ghosts, nor ghastly owls do flee.

But friendly fairies, met with many Graces
And lightfoot nymphs, can chase the lingering night
With hay-de-guys and trimly trodden traces,
Whilst sisters nine, which dwell on Parnass' height,
Do make them music for their more delight;
And Pan himself, to kiss their crystal faces,
Will pipe and dance, when Phoebe shineth bright:
Such peerless pleasures have we in these places.

Colin

And I, whilst youth and course of careless years
Did let me walk withouten links of love,
In such delights did joy among my peers.
But riper age such pleasures doth reprove,
My fancy eke from former follies move
To stayed steps: for time in passing wears
(As garments doen, which waxen old above),
And draweth new delights with hoary hairs.

Tho couth I sing of love, and tune my pipe
Unto my plaintive pleas in verses made:
Tho would I seek for queen apples unripe
To give my Rosalind, and in summer shade
Dight gaudy garlands, was my common trade,
To crown her golden locks; but years more ripe,
And loss of her whose love as life I weigh'd,
Those weary wanton toys away did wipe.

Hobbinoll

Colin, to hear thy rhymes and roundelays
Which thou wert wont on wasteful hills to sing
I more delight, than lark in summer days:
Whose echo made the neighbour groves to ring,
And taught the birds, which in the lower spring
Did shroud in shady leaves from sunny rays,
Frame to thy song their cheerful chirruping,
Or hold their peace for shame of thy sweet lays.

I saw Calliope, with Muses mo,
Soon as thy oaten pipe began to sound,
Their ivory lutes and tambourines forgo,
And from the fountain where they sat around
Run after hastily thy silver sound.
But when they came where thou thy skill didst show,

They drew aback, as half with shame confound
Shepherd to see, them in their art outgo.

Colin

Of Muses, Hobbinoll, I con no skill,
For they bene daughters of the highest Jove
And holden scorn of homely shepherd's quill.
For sith I heard that Pan with Phoebus strove,
Which him to much rebuke and danger drove,
I never list presume to Parnass hill;
But piping low in shade of lowly grove,
I play to please myself, all be it ill.

Nought weigh I who my song doth praise or blame,
Ne strive to win renown, or pass the rest.
With shepherd sits not follow flying fame
But feed his flock in fields, where falls hem best.
I wot my rhymes bene rough and rudely drest;
The fitter they my careful case to frame.
Enough is me to paint out my unrest
And pour my piteous plaints out in the same.

The God of shepherds, Tityrus, is dead,
Who taught me homely, as I can, to make.
He whilst he lived was the sovereign head
Of shepherds all that bene with love y-take.
Well couth he wail his woes, and lightly slake
The flames which love within his heart had bred,
And tell us merry tales, to keep us wake
The while our sheep about us safely fed.

Now dead is he, and lieth wrapt in lead
(O why should death on him such outrage show?),
And all his passing skill with him is fled,
The fame whereof doth daily greater grow.
But if on me some little drops would flow

Of that the spring was in his learned head,
I soon would learn these woods to wail my woe,
And teach the trees their trickling tears to shed.

Then should my plaints, caus'd of discourtesy,
As messengers of all my woeful plight,
Fly to my love, wherever that she be,
And pierce her heart with point of worthy wite
As she deserves, that wrought so deadly spite.
And thou, Menalcas, that by treachery
Didst underfong my lass to wax so light,
Shouldst well be known for such thy villainy.

But since I am not as I wish I were,
Ye gentle shepherds, which your flocks do feed
Whether on hills or dales or other where,
Bear witness all of this so wicked deed:
And tell the lass whose flower is wox a weed,
And faultless faith is turned to faithless fere,
That she the truest shepherd's heart made bleed
That lives on earth, and loved her most dear.

Hobbinoll

O careful Colin, I lament thy case!
Thy tears would make the hardest flint to flow.
Ah faithless Rosalind, and void of grace,
That art the root of all this ruthful woe!
But now is time, I guess, homeward to go:
Then rise, ye blessed flocks, and home apace,
Lest night with stealing steps do you forslow
And wet your tender lambs, that by you trace.

Colin's Emblem

Già speme spenta

2 *shades* shady places *weaned* 'weaned away', drawn away *wandering* i.e. *once* wandering, before I found this place

3 *what wants me* what is lacking to me

4 *simple* pure, clear *warbling* singing, murmuring

6 *dainty* pretty, graceful (OED 4) *dight* arrayed, adorned (OED 10)

8 'Attune their songs perfectly to the sound of the water's fall'

9 *bless* praise, extol (OED 5b)

10 i.e., You are in the 'state of innocence', of inner peace and purity, in which man lived before Adam and Eve's fall. Pastoral literature often assumes that shepherds or rustics still retain something of this happy state.

12 *withouten* without *bene* infinitive of *be* *y-tost* tossed, scattered—hence disturbed, agitated (OED 5) The *Calendar* is full of such archaisms, dialect-forms, rustic-sounding affixes and coinages.

13 *lays* songs *boast* display, exercise: unusual non-pejorative use

16 *shroud* shelter (cf.10.551) *pate* head

17 *list* wish to

18 *bewitch* commonly 'fascinate, attract'; but here perhaps 'harm, as under an evil spell'

19 *Leave me* the old ethical dative: 'Leave for my sake', 'Leave as I tell you' *harbrough* harbour, shelter *nis* is not

20 *brere* See 9.19n. *witch* wych-elm, with *winding* (pliant or sinuous) branches used to make bows. The holly, briar and wych-elm all grow in inhospitable country: these bare hills lack even such vegetation.

22 *bene* archaic plural of *be*

23 *night-ravens* night-birds, variously identified: 'tokens' of 'all misfortunes' (E.K.)

24 *elvish ghosts* fairy or supernatural spirits *flee* fly, roam

25-32 Shows traces of Horace, *Odes* I.iv. But note the admixture of local English and classical mythologies—as of classical and English names of shepherds right through the *Calendar*.

25 *met with* together with, assembled along with
many Graces Strictly speaking, there were three Graces; but as E.K. says, the word was loosely applied to the spirits of many 'gifts of bounty'.

26 *chase the lingering night* 'drive out the last traces of night', i.e. revel till daybreak

27 *hay-de-guy(s)* a country dance *trimly trodden* neatly or prettily danced-out *traces* dance steps (OED 3)

28 *sisters nine* the nine Muses, goddesses of poetry
Parnass Parnassus, the Greek mountain sacred to Apollo and the Muses

29 *more* i.e., greater

30 *Pan* the chief classical god of the woods or of all nature
crystal clear, fair

31 *Phoebe* Diana the moon-goddess; hence the moon

33 *careless* carefree

34 *walk* go about, love (OED 4, 6) *links* bonds, chains

35 *joy* rejoice, live in joy *peers* fellows, companions

36 But as the context shows, Colin has not outgrown love with age: he is still in love, and suffering thereby.

37 *fancy* love, especially the light love of youth; or perhaps more generally 'desire, taste, inclination' (OED A8)
eke also *move* linked to *doth*, 1.36: 'riper age doth move my fancy from former follies to stayed steps'.

38 *stayed* restrained, controlled *wears* wears out, exhausts: unusual use, without a clear object

39 *doen, waxen* plurals of *do, wax* (cf. *bene*, 1.22)
wax grow *old above* probably 'over-old, too old'

40 *draweth* induces, brings on (OED 30)
new delights i.e., more sober or spiritual pleasures

41 *Tho* then *couth* knew how to, had the skill to (past tense of *can*, to know: OED 3)

43 *queen apples* an early-growing variety of apple. Even this is sent unripe, showing the lover's impetuosity.

44 *summer shade* the shade of a tree in the hot summer

45 *dight* (to) frame, make (OED 7)

47 *loss* in love, not death: see ll.109 ff. *weighed* measured, valued

48 *weary* wearisome, dull (OED 6); or perhaps 'fatiguing' (OED 5) *toys* trifles, frivolities *wipe* efface, remove

49 *roundelay(s)* a short song with a refrain, like that in 'August' in the *Calendar*

50 *wont* accustomed *wasteful* barren, desolate (OED 3)

51 *than lark* i.e., than to hear a lark singing

52 *whose* referring to Colin's songs *neighbour* neighbouring, nearby

53 *lower* i.e., in the valley *spring* 'wood . . . of young trees springing' (OED 10: so also E.K.)

54 *shroud* shelter (l.16) *sunny* of the sun, solar

55 *frame* fashion, adapt

56 *for shame of* put to shame by

57 *Calliope* The Muse of epic, hence sometimes considered the chief Muse *mo* more, other

58 *oaten* made from an oat-stem (contrast *ivory*, l.59)

59 *tambourine(s)* a musical instrument, earlier called 'timbrel'. (OED first cites from this passage.)

60 *the fountain* no doubt the Castalian spring on Parnassus (see l.70n)

63 *confound* 'confounded', confused, amazed

65 *con* know *Jove* Jupiter

66–7 *bene, holden* plurals of *be, hold*

67 *quill* (a) pipe (OED 1c); (b) pen (OED 3b)

68 *sith* since *Pan with Phoebus strove* See Ovid, *Metamorphoses* XI. 153-71. *Phoebus* Apollo

69 *him* i.e., Pan *danger* harm, damage (OED 6)

70 *list* desired *presume* aspire proudly *Parnass hill* Parnassus, the mountain sacred to Apollo and the Muses

71 *low* softly *lowly* low: in a valley as opposed to 'Parnass hill'. Both words suggest humility.

72 *all be it* although it be *ill* bad, harsh

73 *Nought weigh I* I do not at all consider

74 *Ne* nor *pass* surpass, excel over

75 *sits not* is not fit or proper (OED 17), with 'to' understood before 'follow' *flying* fleeting, transient

76 *falls* fits (OED 33) *hem* old equivalent of *them*—i.e., the shepherd and / or his flock

77 *wot* know *bene* cf.ll.22, 66 *rudely drest* crudely fashioned

78 *careful* sorrowful, full of care *frame* express (OED 8)

79 *Enough is me* It is enough for me *paint out* depict, express

80 *the same* i.e., these verses

81 *Tityrus* A shepherd in Virgil's Eclogues, identified with Virgil himself. Hence applied to other great poets: here, as E.K. notes, to Chaucer.

82 *homely* adverb: plainly, crudely *can* know, have the skill *make* compose poetry (OED 5)

84 *bene* cf. ll.22, 66 *y-take* 'taken', captured, seized: used specially of diseases and magic spells (OED *take* 7)

85 *couth* knew how to (cf.l.41)

89 *lead* i.e., a lead coffin

90 *outrage* 'violent injury or harm' (OED 3)

91 *passing* surpassing

94 *that the spring was* that (i.e., his poetic genius) of which the source was

95 *learn* teach

97 *caused of* caused by *discourtesy* harshness, cruelty: a very strong sense. Gracious love, like other gracious conduct, was among the virtues of courtly life.

100 *point of worthy wite* 'the prick (i.e., sting, smart) of deserved blame' (E.K.) *wite* blame, reproach

101 *wrought* worked, practised *so deadly spite* such deadly hatred or cruelty

102 *Menalcas* clearly the shepherd who has stolen Rosalind's love

103 *underfong* 'undermine and deceive by false suggestion' (E.K.) *wax* grow, become *light* fickle, light-of-love

105 *as I wish I were* i.e., as gifted as Tityrus

107 *other where* elsewhere

108 *this so wicked deed* such a wicked deed

109 *flower . . . weed* love is turned to scorn or hatred (*wox* waxed: grown, become)

110 *faultless* flawless, pure *fere* companion, comrade

113 *careful* cf. l.78

114 *flow* melt (OED 2)

116 *ruthful* piteous (*ruth* pity)

119 *stealing* soft, stealthy *forslow* delay, hold up (OED 2)

120 *wet* i.e., wet the fleeces with dew *trace* go, walk (OED 1)

121 *Colin's Emblem* Each eclogue of the *Calendar* ends with one or more 'emblems' (symbols or representations, hence mottos) appropriate to the characters.

122 *Già speme spenta* (Italian) 'Hope is quite spent'. The January motto had been '*Ancora speme*', 'There is still hope'.

Michael Drayton

11 : The Daffodil Song

[In 1606, Drayton published a radically revised version of the pastorals brought out in 1593 as *The Shepherd's Garland*. He added a new eclogue (no.IX) describing a shearing-supper and song-contest in the Cotswolds. This and the next poem are the first two of three songs sung there, in rising complexity of theme. (They had earlier come out separately in *England's Helicon* in 1600.)

The Daffodil Song conveys the quintessential delicacy of the Elizabethan lyric at its simplest, with a childlike confusion between the maiden Daffodil and the flower. The second poem has more elaborate, more obviously patterned conceits. Each poem is sung by two shepherds in alternate speeches—one of the standard modes of such song-contests.]

Batte Gorbo, as thou cam'st this way
By yonder little hill,
Or as thou through the fields didst stray,
Saw'st thou my Daffadil?

She's in a frock of Lincoln green,
Which colour likes her sight,
And never hath her beauty seen
But through a veil of white:

Than roses richer to behold
That trim up lover's bowers,
The pansy and the marigold,
Though Phoebus' paramours.

Gorbo Thou well describ'st the daffadil:

It is not full an hour
Since by the spring, near yonder hill,
I saw that lovely flower.

Batte Yet my fair flower thou didst not meet,
Nor news of her didst bring:
And yet my Daffadil's more sweet
Than that by yonder spring.

Gorbo I saw a shepherd that doth keep
In yonder field of lilies,
Was making, as he fed his sheep,
A wreath of daffadillies.

Batte Yet, Gorbo, thou delud'st me still:
My flower thou didst not see.
For know, my pretty Daffadil
Is worn of none but me.

To show itself but near her seat
No lily is so bold,
Except to shade her from the heat
Or keep her from the cold.

Gorbo Through yonder vale as I did pass,
Descending from the hill,
I met a smirking bonny lass:
They call her Daffadil:

Whose presence, as along she went,
The pretty flowers did greet
As though their heads they downward bent
With homage to her feet.

And all the shepherds that were nigh,
From top of every hill,

Unto the valleys loud did cry:
'There goes sweet Daffadil.'

Batte Ay, gentle shepherd, now with joy
Thou all my flocks dost fill.
That's she alone, kind shepherd's boy:
Let us to Daffadil.

4 *Daffadil* A common old variant.
5 *Lincoln green* a bright green material, originally made at Lincoln (compared to the daffodil's leaves)
6 *likes her sight* (a) pleases her sight (b) suits her appearance (*like*, to please, to suit: OED 1)
7 'Never lets her beauty be seen'
8 *white* like petals. The common daffodil, of course, is yellow.
9 'Richer to behold than roses'
10 *trim up* adorn
12 *Phoebus* Helios or Apollo, the sun-god. These flowers are said to be his *paramours* (love-partners) presumably as liking heat and turning to the sun: true of the marigold but not so much of the pansy.
21 *keep* stay, be present (OED 38)
23 *fed* i.e., grazed, let feed
29 'Even to appear where she is'
32 *keep* protect (OED 14)
35 *smirking* smiling: hence neat, trim, pretty. No pejorative sense.
37-8 Inversion: The flowers greeted her presence.
37-40 i.e., She trod the flowers as she went. By skilful pathetic fallacy, this becomes a scene of harmony rather than destruction.
47 *That's she alone* i.e., The description fits her alone.
48 *Let us to* Let us go to

12 : 'Tell me, thou skilful shepherd's swain'

[See headnote to the previous poem.]

Motto Tell me, thou skilful shepherd's swain,
Who's yonder in the valley set?

Perkin O it is she whose sweets do stain
The lily, rose, the violet.

Motto Why doth the sun, against his kind,
Stay his bright chariot in the skies?
Perkin He pauseth, almost strooken blind,
With gazing on her heavenly eyes.

Motto Why do thy flocks forbear their food,
Which sometime was their chief delight?
Perkin Because they need no other good,
That live in presence of her sight.

Motto How come those flowers to flourish still,
Not withering with sharp winter's breath?
Perkin She hath robb'd Nature of her skill,
And comforts all things with her breath.

Motto Why slide these brooks so slow away,
As swift as the wild roe that were?
Perkin O muse not, shepherd, that they stay,
When they her heavenly voice do hear.

Motto From whence come all these goodly swains
And lovely girls attir'd in green?
Perkin From gathering garlands on the plains
To crown thy Syl, our shepherd's queen.

Motto The sun that lights this world below,
Flocks, brooks, and flowers, can witness bear,
Perkin These shepherds and these nymphs do know,
Thy Sylvia is as chaste as fair.

1 *skilful* viz., in song
2 *set* sitting (OED 5)
3 *sweets* graces, 'sweetnesses' *stain* darken by contrast, eclipse (OED 1b)
5 *against his kind* contrary to his nature

6 *stay* stop, hold back *chariot* of the Sun-God
5–6 i.e., The sun is not setting at the appointed time.
7 *strooken* struck: old participial form
7–8 i.e., Her bright eyes dazzle the sun itself.
9 *forbear* forgo, hold back from
10 *sometime* once
11 *good* benefit, blessing
13 *flourish* flower, blossom (the literal sense: Latin *flos*, flower)
15 *skill* art, expertise—hence ascribed task or the power to perform it
16 *comforts* strengthens, invigorates (OED 4)
18 'that were once as swift as the roe' (a small deer)
19 *muse* ask, wonder (OED 2)
21 *goodly swains* handsome shepherds

Sir Philip Sidney

Astrophil and Stella

[This sequence of 108 sonnets and 11 'songs' was composed *c.* 1582 and published in 1591. It did much to popularize the love-sonnet cycle in English. Astrophil ('star-lover') represents Sidney and Stella ('star') Penelope Devereux, daughter of the Earl of Essex. She had already married Lord Rich in 1581. Astrophil laments his frustration in many sonnets, and punningly castigates Lord Rich in two (nos. 24, 37); but the sequence does not present the finished story of a thwarted love, as sometimes suggested. It seems better to read it as a series of vivid records of the various aspects of love. Their vivacity sometimes anticipates the Metaphysical poets, and brings many conventional Petrarchan situations to life.

These sonnets have a variety of rhyme-schemes, ranging from pure Italian to pure English. Interesting variations have been pointed out in the notes.]

13 Sonnet 6: 'Some lovers speak'

[The poet mocks and rejects conventional love-poetry and professes simple, sincere speech; but this was itself a convention. Cf. *Astrophil and Stella* Sonnet 1.

The form is Italian, inclining towards English in the rhyme-scheme of ll.1-8.]

Some lovers speak, when they their Muses entertain,
Of hopes begot by fear, of wot not what desires,
Of force of heavenly beams infusing hellish pain,
Of living deaths, dear wounds, fair storms, and freezing
fires.

Some one his song in Jove and Jove's strange tales attires,
Broder'd with bulls and swans, powder'd with golden rain;
Another, humbler wit to shepherd's pipe retires,
Yet hiding royal blood full oft in rural vein.
To some, a sweetest plaint a sweetest style affords
While tears pour out his ink, and sighs breathe out his words:
His paper pale despair, and pain his pen doth move.
I can speak what I feel, and feel as much as they,
But think that all the map of my state I display
When trembling voice brings forth that I do Stella love.

1 *entertain* receive as a guest (*entertain the Muse*, write poetry)
2–4 Standard Petrarchan paradoxes
2 *wot not* (I) do not know
3 *heavenly beams* i.e., the light of the mistress's eyes
infusing instilling, imparting
4 *dear wounds* prized or welcome wounds *fair* i.e., fair-weather
5–6 Refers to treatments of love in erotic-mythological epyllia (see Introduction, pp. 21–22)
Jove or Jupiter wooed his human loves in many disguises: a bull (Europa), a swan (Leda), a shower of gold (Danaë).
5 *attires* dresses, adorns
6 *broder'd* embroidered *powder'd* spangled (OED 3)
7–8 Pastoral poetry often conveyed courtly allusions and a sophisticated sensibility.
8 *vein* pun on the literal and metaphorical senses
10–11 Such personifications were another common convention.
10 *pour out* dissolve, cause to flow; or perhaps 'pour out as', 'act as'
11 i.e., Despair is the paper on which he writes.
pain . . . pen an inept but not impossible pun
13 *map* chart, guide, picture

14 Sonnet 20: 'Fly, fly, my friends'

[A strikingly dramatic version of the hackneyed fancy of Cupid's golden arrow that induces love. Shows Sidney's genius for bringing stale conventions to life.]

Fly, fly, my friends! I have my death-wound—fly!
See there that boy, that murd'ring boy I say,
Who, like a thief, hid in dark bush doth lie,
Till bloody bullet get him wrongful prey.
So tyrant he no fitter place could spy
Nor so fair level in so secret stay
As that sweet black which veils the heavenly eye:
There himself with his shot he close doth lay.
Poor passenger, pass now thereby I did,
And stay'd, pleas'd with the prospect of the place,
While that black hue from me the bad guest hid.
But straight I saw motions of lightning grace,
    And then descried the glist'ring of his dart:
    But ere I could fly thence, it pierc'd my heart.

1 *death-wound* mortal wound 2 *boy* i.e., Cupid
4 *bloody* i.e., spilling blood (OED 4)
bullet earlier, any missile—but only rarely an arrow
6 *so fair level* such easy aim
so secret stay such a fine hiding-place
7 *sweet black which veils* i.e., Stella's eyelashes—the 'bush' in which Cupid has hidden. Stella's glances are Cupid's arrows, inspiring love (see ll.12–14)
8 *shot* i.e., arrow (OED 13) *close* hidden (OED 4)
lay lie: accepted Elizabethan usage
9 *thereby* 'by there', nearby
10 *stay'd* stopped, lingered
prospect view, scene (i.e., Stella's beauty)
11 *black* of the eyelashes; but metaphorically 'evil, treacherous'
guest perhaps 'stranger' (OED 2)
12 *of lightning grace* quick and graceful as lightning
13 *glist'ring* glint, glitter (of the golden arrow)

15 Sonnet 31: 'With how sad steps'

[Perhaps inspired by *Lydia,* an old Latin poem once ascribed to Virgil: 'O Moon, thou knowest what grief is: pity one who grieves.' (Ringler, citing J.B. Leishman) The moon is the set symbol of inconstancy, because of its changing phases. Here, in a poignant reversal of convention, it stands for the faithful lover.]

With how sad steps, O Moon, thou climb'st the skies!
How silently, and with how wan a face!
What, may it be that even in heavenly place
That busy archer his sharp arrows tries?
Sure, if that long-with-love-acquainted eyes
Can judge of love, thou feel'st a lover's case.
I read it in thy looks: thy languisht grace,
To me that feel the like, thy state descries.
Then even of fellowship, O Moon, tell me,
Is constant love deem'd there but want of wit?
Are beauties there as proud as here they be?
Do they above love to be lov'd, and yet
        Those lovers scorn whom that love doth possess?
        Do they call virtue there, ungratefulness?

4 *busy* restless, meddlesome (cf. 'busybody')
archer i.e., Cupid. See no. 14.
tries practises, tries out
6 *feels'st* (a) experience yourself (b) feel for, sympathize with
case state, condition (OED 5)
7 *languisht* wilting, fainting
8 *descries* discloses, reveals (OED 2)
9 *of* out of, because of
10 *wit* intelligence, wisdom
14 Inversion: 'Do they call ungratefulness a virtue there?'
ungratefulness: in not responding to offered love: ungraciousness, harshness

16 Sonnet 41: 'Having this day my horse, my lance'

[Like the knights of old romance, Astrophil declares himself inspired by his love in the tournament in which he is fighting. But this conventional situation is authenticated by the fact that Sidney played a leading part in the revival of chivalric pageantry in Elizabeth's day.]

Having this day my horse, my hand, my lance
Guided so well that I obtain'd the prize
Both by the judgement of the English eyes,
And of some sent from that sweet enemy, France:
Horsemen my skill in horsemanship advance,
Townfolks my strength; a daintier judge applies
His praise to sleight which from good use doth rise;
Some lucky wits impute it but to chance;
Others, because of both sides I do take
My blood from them who did excel in this,
Think Nature me a man-at-arms did make.
How far they shoot awry! The true cause is,
    Stella look'd on, and from her heavenly face
    Sent forth the beams which made so fair my race.

4 i.e., The tournament was held to honour some guests from France. *sweet enemy* A stock Petrarchan phrase for the mistress, but here applied to politics. *Sweet* presumably refers to the refinements of French courtly culture, and *enemy* to the traditional hostility between England and France. There may be specific reference to the erstwhile proposal, which Sidney and his party opposed, that Elizabeth should marry the French Duke of Alençon. This would make the Petrarchan phrase specially appropriate.

5 *advance* praise (OED 5)

6 *townfolks* i.e., ignorant tradesmen or workmen
daintier more subtle or perceptive (OED *dainty* 5)
applies turns, directs

7 *sleight* skill *use* practice

8 *lucky* fortunate, gifted: obviously ironic, specially in view of their own belief in luck or fortune.

9 *of both sides* i.e., the father's and mother's

take my blood from descend from. Sidney's aristocratic lineage was richer on his mother's side, his maternal uncle being the great Earl of Leicester.

11 *Nature* The agent said to bestow inborn gifts or powers: opposed to Fortune, which affords external or chance gifts only.

12 *shoot awry* miss the mark, miss the truth

14 *beams* her eyes' radiance *fair* successful (*a fair day*, a success in battle: (OED 14b) *race* 'a course in a tournament' (OED 4a)

17 Sonnet 72: 'Desire, though thou my old companion art'

[Presents in vivid, dramatic terms the conflict between carnal love ('Desire') and a higher, more worshipful adoration of the mistress ('pure love').]

Desire, though thou my old companion art,
And oft so cling'st to my pure love that I
One from the other scarcely can descry,
While each doth blow the fire of my heart,
Now from thy fellowship I needs must part:
Venus is taught with Dian's wings to fly.
I must no more in thy sweet passions lie:
Virtue's gold now must head my Cupid's dart.
Service and honour, wonder with delight,
Fear to offend, will worthy to appear,
Care shining in mine eyes, faith in my sprite:
These things are left me by my only dear.
    But thou, Desire, because thou wouldst have all,
    Now banish'd art— but yet, alas, how shall?

3 *descry* distinguish, discriminate (OED 7b: very rare use)

6 Venus is the goddess of love, Diana of virginity or chastity;

wings suggests Cupid. Erotic love itself has grown chaste and spiritualized, as suggested in ll.2–3 and indeed to the end, in l.14. The conflict conceals a subtler interaction.

7 *lie* (a) rest (b) utter falsehoods (i.e., the false conventions of love-poetry)

8 *virtue's gold* rather than the love-inducing gold of Cupid's usual arrow: the myth has been transformed by the new spiritual context. *head* tip

9 *service* of the mistress, in love *honour* (a) reverence for the mistress (b) honourable or virtuous conduct *wonder* 'profound admiration' (OED 7c)

10 *will . . . appear* the determination to appear worthy

11 *care* worry, distress *faith* steadfast love, rather than confidence of success *sprite* spirit

13 *wouldst have all* i.e., leave no room for these superior virtues

14 *shall* i.e., shall be banished

18 : 'Leave me, O love'

[This poem is *not* part of *Astrophil and Stella,* though sometimes misguidedly appended to it by later editors, distorting the entire nature of the sequence. It was composed before *Astrophil and Stella,* so cannot mark a permanent rejection of that or any other love-poetry.]

Leave me, O love, which reachest but to dust,
And thou my mind, aspire to higher things.
Grow rich in that which never taketh rust:
Whatever fades, but fading pleasure brings.
Draw in thy beams, and humble all thy might
To that sweet yoke where lasting freedoms be,
Which breaks the clouds and opens forth the light
That doth both shine and give us sight to see.
O take fast hold: let that light be thy guide
In this small course which birth draws out to death,
And think how evil becometh him to slide

Who seeketh heaven and comes of heavenly breath.
Then farewell, world! thy uttermost I see:
Eternal Love, maintain thy life in me.

1 *which . . . dust* Probably a particularizing, not a generalizing statement: 'that particular kind of love (i.e., erotic love) which reaches' etc. Contrast 'eternal love' (1.14).

3 Echoes Matthew 6:20: 'But lay up for yourselves treasures in heaven, where neither moth nor rust doth corrupt.' Cf. James 5:3.

5 *beams* of light: see 1.7n.

6 *sweet yoke* i.e., service to God. A holy reworking of the Petrarchan oxymoron, as also in the idea of a *yoke* conferring *lasting freedoms.*

7 *breaks the clouds* like the sun, once the human soul's own proud 'beams' have been suppressed

10 *course* 'life viewed as a race that is run' (OED 17)

11 *how evil becometh him* how ill it suits him
slide lapse, fall (from virtue)

12 *comes of heavenly breath* God breathed life into man (Genesis 2:7)

13 *uttermost* full extent, through and through

14 *maintain thy life* i.e., live, dwell

Edmund Spenser

Amoretti

[*Amoretti* (published 1595) contains 89 sonnets followed by four occasional poems, culminating in the 'Epithalamion'. The sonnets record Spenser's courtship of Elizabeth Boyle, his future wife (some of them might have been composed earlier); the 'Epithalamion' (Greek 'marriage song') celebrates their union. The earlier sonnets alternate between two veins, both Petrarchan in their respective ways: pronounced idealization of love and of the beloved, and complaints of her scorn and 'tyranny'. A change comes with Sonnet 62: the mistress has now granted her love, and the remaining poems commemorate a secure love and eventual marriage.

Amoretti (Italian) means 'little loves' — i.e., the 'infant Cupid' figures common in Renaissance art and imagery. Such infant Cupids are imagined to flutter in the mistress's glances (Sonnet 16). By a fanciful extension, the sonnets are themselves seen as so many attendant Cupids.

The sonnets of *Amoretti* vary the standard English pattern by making the second rhyme of each quatrain the first rhyme of the next: i.e, the pattern is *abab bcbc cdcd ee.*]

19 Sonnet 3: 'The sovereign beauty'

[An extreme instance of spiritual idealization of the beloved in terms of Christian Neo-Platonism. The lover is also spiritually elevated as a result. The underlying philosophy is brought out in Spenser's 'An Hymn in Honour of Love'.]

The sovereign beauty which I do admire,
Witness the world how worthy to be prais'd,
The light whereof hath kindled heavenly fire

In my frail spirit, by her from baseness rais'd:
That, being now with her huge brightness daz'd,
Base thing I can no more endure to view,
But looking still on her, I stand amaz'd
At wondrous sight of so celestial hue.
So when my tongue would speak her praises due,
It stopped is with thought's astonishment;
And when my pen would write her titles true,
It ravisht is with fancy's wonderment.
Yet in my heart I then both speak and write
The wonder that my wit cannot indite.

1 *sovereign* supreme
2 'Let the world bear witness how worthy of praise she is'
4 *frail* weak, sinful
5 *huge* unusual use indicating degree or intensity, not size
7 *still* always
8 *hue* form, appearance: the original sense
10 *astonishment* paralysis, inertness: the original sense
12 *ravisht* entranced: hence dazed, stupefied
fancy as then understood, the power of creating poetic or other images *wonderment* i.e., awestruck stupor
14 *wit* intelligence; here, the poetic faculty in particular

20 Sonnet 10: 'Unrighteous Lord of Love'

[In contrast to the last poem, this one is a standard complaint of the scorned lover, full of conventional images. It is loosely based on Petrarch, *Rime* 121, rendered by Wyatt as 'Behold, Love, thy power how she despiseth!']

Unrighteous Lord of Love, what law is this
That me thou makest thus tormented be,
The whiles she lordeth in licentious bliss
Of her free will, scorning both thee and me!
See how the tyranness doth joy to see

The huge massacres which her eyes do make,
And humbled hearts brings captives unto thee,
That thou of them may'st mighty vengeance take.
But her proud heart do thou a little shake,
And that high look, with which she doth control
All the world's pride, bow to a baser make,
And all her fault in thy black book enrol:
That I may laugh at her in equal sort
As she doth laugh at me, and makes my pain her sport.

1 *unrighteous* unjust *Lord of Love* i.e., Cupid
Love . . . law Note the ironic association: 'love' should be above 'law'

3 *the whiles* while *lordeth* dominates, 'lords it'
licentious unrestrained, lawless

4 *of her free will* i.e, unchecked, unrestrained
scorning both thee and me i.e., She spurns not only this lover but all thought of love.

7 *brings captives* brings as captives

8 *vengeance* loosely used: harsh or cruel treatment. The God of Love should not seek revenge on lovers.

9 *shake* i.e., disturb, impair confidence

10-11 *control . . . pride* (a) command, or have at her disposal, the finest things in the world (OED *pride* 5); (b) curb all men's pride

11 *bow* transitive: make it bow *make* mate, partner
i.e., Let her love one inferior to herself.

12 *black book* a fancied book where Cupid records all those who have offended him by scorning love

13 *in equal sort* in the same way

14 Note the metrical variation: an alexandrine or six-foot line.

21 Sonnet 65: 'The doubt which ye misdeem'

[By this time, the poet has won his mistress's love, and the sonnets strike a more intimate note of mutual love. Here, in ll.9-14, love is idealized in personal rather than philosophic or spiritual terms.]

The doubt which ye misdeem, fair love, is vain,
That fondly fear to lose your liberty,
When losing one, two liberties ye gain,
And make him bond that bondage erst did fly.
Sweet be the bands, the which true love doth tie
Without constraint or dread of any ill:
The gentle bird feels no captivity
Within her cage, but sings and feeds her fill.
There pride dare not approach, nor discord spill
The league 'twixt them that loyal love hath bound,
But simple truth and mutual good-will
Seeks with sweet peace to salve each other's wound.
 There Faith doth fearless dwell in brazen tower,
 And spotless Pleasure builds her sacred bower.

1 *doubt* fear
misdeem wrongly hold or judge
vain idle, baseless
2 *fondly* foolishly
3 *two liberties* i.e., She will retain her own liberty and also control her lover's.
4 *bond* one held in bondage: a slave (OED 3)
bondage . . . fly i.e., previously shunned love
5 *bands* bonds
6 *without constraint* without force or coercion. The lovers willingly submit to each other's bondage.
ill evil, harm
7 *gentle* tame (OED 4b); but surely implying 'noble, hence fit for refined love'. Italian *gentil* was commonly used in this sense.
9 *There* i.e. in the state of true love *spill* destroy (OED 4)
10 *league* bond, alliance *'twixt* betwixt, between
11 *simple* pure; but also single, unified (OED 11)
12 *peace* concord, amity (OED 4)
salve heal, soothe
wound sorrow; or perhaps the earlier 'pang' from Cupid's arrow
13 *in brazen tower* i.e., impregnably
14 *spotless* 'without spot', stainless

22 Sonnet 68: 'Most glorious Lord of Life'

[An Easter sonnet addressed to Christ: love of God and Christian charity — i.e., love of men in the sight of God, because God loves them — blend into amorous love.

Petrarch first saw Laura during an Easter service in church, and has Easter sonnets in different veins (*Rime* nos. 3, 62, 211.) Precedents have also been found in the French poets Du Bellay and Desportes.]

Most glorious Lord of Life, that on this day
Didst make thy triumph over death and sin
And, having harrow'd hell, didst bring away
Captivity thence captive, us to win:
This joyous day, dear Lord, with joy begin,
And grant that we, for whom thou diddest die,
Being with thy dear blood clean wash'd from sin,
May live for ever in felicity;
And that thy love we weighing worthily,
May likewise love thee for the same again,
And for thy sake that all like dear didst buy,
With love may one another entertain.
So let us love, dear love, like as we ought:
Love is the lesson which the Lord us taught.

2 Christ redeemed man from the original sin caused by Adam and Eve's disobedience. Death was commonly a figure of damnation. The idea is made vivid in Milton's presentation of Sin and Death (*Paradise Lost* II.648 ff.)

3–4 Between crucifixion and resurrection, Christ was thought to have entered hell, chained the devil, and brought out from there certain key Biblical figures like Adam, Abel, Noah, Moses, Abraham and David. Thus man's *captivity* to evil, or damnation, was itself checked or made *captive*. The phrase echoes Judges 5:12 and Ephesians 4:8.

4 *win* save, redeem (OED 8) — but suggesting the spoils of war. Cf. *harrow* (l.3) = harry, rob.

7 *dear* (a) beloved (b) precious. The line echoes Revelation 1:5.

9 *weighing* measuring, valuing *worthily* at its true worth
11 *all . . . buy* redeemed (*buy*: OED 4) all of us with equal love; or, bought at equal cost. An interesting deviation from the doctrine of election, that God saved some and damned others, as strongly professed by most radical Protestants like Spenser.
12 *entertain* treat, receive (OED 7, 14)
13 *dear love* Now addressing the mistress *like as* as
13–14 Cf. John 15:12, Ephesians 5:2.

23 Sonnet 73: 'Being my self captived here'

[Another intimate, non-philosophic sonnet, expanding the bird imagery of **21**.7–8. Closely based on a sonnet by Torquato Tasso (*Rime* no. 222).]

Being my self captived here in care,
My heart, whom none with servile bands can tie
But the fair tresses of your golden hair,
Breaking his prison, forth to you doth fly.
Like as a bird that in one's hand doth spy
Desired food, to it doth make its flight,
Even so my heart, that wont on your fair eye
To feed his fill, flies back unto your sight.
Do you him take, and in your bosom bright
Gently encage, that he may be your thrall:
Perhaps he there may learn, with rare delight,
To sing your name and praises over all:
    That it hereafter may you not repent
    Him lodging in your bosom to have lent.

1 *my self* contrasted with *my heart* (l.2)
captived held captive *care* sorrow, suffering
2 *servile bands* bonds of servitude
3 *your . . . hair* as the lover's bonds: a common conceit. Cf. Sonnet 37.

4 *his prison* i.e., the body
7 *wont* was accustomed
8 *your sight* i.e., the sight of you
9 *Do you him take* take him *bright* beautiful, fair (OED 3)
10 *thrall* captive
12 *over all* everywhere; or perhaps 'above all others'
13 *that* so that *it . . . repent* old impersonal construction: 'it may not repent you' (OED 2) — i.e., you may not repent or regret
14 *lent* granted, afforded (OED 2)

Samuel Daniel

Delia

[Daniel's *Delia* (1592) is one of the most successful, though most conventional, sonnet-sequences published during the vogue of the form. In 1544 the French poet Maurice Scève had published a highly philosophic poem-sequence, *Délie*, where the mistress was viewed as an embodiment of the Platonic Idea. (*Délie* is an anagram of *L'Idée* or 'the Idea'.) Daniel borrows the name but not the philosophy.]

24 Sonnet 5: 'Whilst Youth and Error'

[This sonnet uses the Actaeon myth. Actaeon the hunter surprised Diana bathing. The angry goddess turned him into a hart, and he was torn by his own hounds. So too the mistress, angered by his intrusion, destroys him by her scorn.]

Whilst Youth and Error led my wand'ring mind
And set my thoughts in heedless ways to range,
All unawares, a goddess chaste I find,
Diana-like, to work my sudden change.
For her no sooner had my view bewray'd,
But with disdain to see me in that place,
With fairest hand, the sweet unkindest maid
Casts water-cold disdain upon my face.
Which turn'd my sport into a hart's despair,
Which is still is chas'd, while I have any breath,
By mine own thoughts: set on me by my fair,
My thoughts, like hounds, pursue me to my death.
    Those that I foster'd of mine own accord
    Are made by her to murder thus their lord.

1 'Youth and 'Error' almost become allegorical figures misleading the poet, as in Morality plays and other moral allegories.
2 *heedless* reckless, dissolute
3 *goddess* i.e., the mistress
4 *Diana* the goddess of chastity. See headnote.
sudden immediate: an obsolete sense (OED 3)
5 *bewray'd* discovered, seen revealed or exposed
8 *water* with which Diana transformed Actaeon
9 *hart* with a conventional pun on *heart*
9–12 Closely echoed in *Twelfth Night* I.i.16-23.
10 *which* i.e., the hart
while . . . breath i.e., as long as I live
11 *fair* i.e., the beautiful woman I love
13 *foster'd* nurtured, brought up *accord* will, desire
13–14 i.e., The very love that he generated for his happiness now torments him.

25 Sonnet 33: 'When men shall find thy flower'

[One of five linked sonnets (nos. 31-35), the last line of one becoming the first line of the next. The theme of undying faith towards a scornful mistress is quintessentially Petrarchan; but the dramatic juxtaposition of old age and love fosters a sense of surprise and deep sincerity.]

When men shall find thy flower, thy glory, pass,
And thou, with careful brow sitting alone,
Received hast this message from thy glass
That tells thee truth, and says that all is gone:
Fresh shalt thou see in me the wounds thou madest,
Though spent thy flame, in me the heat remaining:
I that have lov'd thee thus before thou fadest,
My faith shall wax, when thou art in thy waning.
The world shall find this miracle in me
That fire can burn when all the matter's spent:

Then what my faith hath been thyself shalt see,
And that thou wast unkind, thou may'st repent.
Thou may'st repent that thou hast scorn'd my tears,
When winter snows upon thy sable hairs.

1 *flower* 'bloom', youth (OED 11)
2 *careful* full of care *brow* expression
3 *glass* mirror
6 *flame* of beauty *heat* i.e., the resultant love. Cf. 1.10
8 *wax* grow *wax . . . waning* suggests the moon
11 *thyself shalt see* you will see for yourself
14 *sable* black. An earlier text reads *golden*.

Michael Drayton

Idea

[Drayton first brought out a sonnet-sequence, *Idea's Mirror*, in 1594. But he kept on adding, rejecting, revising and republishing (as *Idea*) long after the sonnet's vogue was over. The final version appeared in 1619.

The sonnets seem directed to Anne Goodere, the daughter of Drayton's patron. But as the name 'Idea' suggests, Drayton's love was highly idealized, even Platonized, to start with. (Cf. the reference to Scève's *L'Idée*, p. 82.) This strain is preserved till 1619, as in the first poem below with its subtle blend of love and spirituality. It dates from 1594 but was revised in 1619. The other two first appeared in 1619. They strike a harder, more realistic and colloquial note, with satire not only of the age (as in Sonnet 6) but of the mistress herself. Sonnet 61 is often taken as the high point of the sequence, with its maturely ironic passion reflected in the lively, intimate matching of personalities.]

26 Sonnet 35: 'Some, misbelieving and profane'

[A subtle blend of love and spirituality. The opening suggests the 'religion of love', half-seriously and half-ironically emulating true religion; but by the end, there is clearly a genuine and total uplift of the spirit.]

Some, misbelieving and profane in love,
When I do speak of miracles by thee,
May say that thou art flattered by me

Who only write my skill in verse to prove.
See miracles, ye unbelieving, see:
A dumb-born muse made to express the mind;
A cripple hand to write, yet lame by kind —
One by thy name, the other touching thee.
Blind were mine eyes till they were seen of thine;
And mine ears deaf, by thy fame healed be;
My vices cur'd by virtues sprung from thee,
My hopes reviv'd, which long in grave had lyne.
  All unclean thoughts, foul spirits, cast out in me
  Only by virtue that proceeds from thee.

2 *miracles* like those wrought by saints
4 *my . . . prove* i.e., hyperbolically, to display my poetic imagination
7 *cripple* earlier used adjectivally: crippled
lame originally applied to any handicap or infirmity
by kind by nature: i.e., born crippled
8 *One . . . the other* the Muse and hand respectively
name . . . touch standard means of working miracles
9 *seen of thine* seen by yours: your gaze cured them (i.e., first 'opened my eyes', taught me beauty and wisdom)
10 *fame* report, reputation
12 *hopes* either of love, or of life's prospects generally: they are like a corpse brought back to life
lyne old variant of *lain*
13 *foul spirits cast out* as saints could do
14 *virtue* no doubt moral and spiritual virtue, but more generally a healing or strengthening power, potency (OED 9b)

27 Sonnet 6: 'How many paltry, foolish, painted things'

How many paltry, foolish, painted things,
That now in coaches trouble every street,
Shall be forgotten, whom no poet sings,

Ere they be well wrapp'd in their winding sheet!
Where I to thee eternity shall give
When nothing else remaineth of these days,
And queens hereafter shall be glad to live
Upon the alms of thy superfluous praise.
Virgins and matrons, reading these my rhymes,
Shall be so much delighted with thy story
That they shall grieve they liv'd not in these times,
To have seen thee, their sex's only glory.
    So shalt thou fly above the vulgar throng,
    Still to survive in my immortal song.

1 *painted things* i.e., women wearing make-up
2 *coaches* new in Elizabethan times (earlier, even women rode on horse-back); hence a sign of degenerate luxury
5 *where* whereas
8 *Upon . . . praise* upon the praise you might give them as alms, left over from your own vast store
10 *story* history, account of life (OED 4e)

28 Sonnet 61: 'Since there's no help'

Since there's no help, come let us kiss and part:
Nay, I have done, you get no more of me.
And I am glad, yea, glad with all my heart,
That thus so cleanly I myself can free.
Shake hands for ever, cancel all our vows,
And when we meet at any time again,
Be it not seen in either of our brows
That we one jot of former love retain.
Now at the last gasp of Love's latest breath,
When, his pulse failing, Passion speechless lies,
When Faith is kneeling by his bed of death,
And Innocence is closing up his eyes,
    Now, if thou would'st, when all have given him over,
    From death to life thou might'st him yet recover.

1 *Since . . . help* i.e., since we cannot remain lovers

2 *done* finished *no more of me* (a) no more of my person, or my company; (b) nothing more out of me. Echoes Chaucer, *Squire's Tale* l. 543.

4 *cleanly* neatly, without fuss or regret

5 *for ever* i.e., as a sign of permanent parting

7 *brows* facial expressions (OED 5b)

9 *latest* last

10 *Passion* clearly = Love (l.9), pictured as a dying man. Ironic variation of the convention whereby the scorned lover dies of love. Here, more robustly, he lets love die.

11 *Faith* in love; but suggests religious faith, personified as the priest attending on a dying man

12 *closing up his eyes* as was done with dying men

11–12 Faith and Innocence are alarmed by the death of love — i.e., the lover is growing inconstant or cynical.

14 *him* i.e., Love. The lover still refuses to grant that he himself is affected!

William Shakespeare

Sonnets

[Shakespeare's Sonnets reflect a relationship, whether real or imaginary, between the poet and a handsome, aristocratic youth or 'Friend'. This develops into a triangular relation between these two and a 'Dark (i.e., dark-haired and dark-eyed) Lady', neither specially beautiful nor constant and virtuous, but of compelling attraction and personality. Indeed, the Sonnets fall into two sequences, one (nos. 1-126) addressed to or relating to the Friend and the other (nos. 127-154) to the Lady.

This much is certain; but the precise history of the relationships remains mysterious, as does the identity of the Friend, the Lady and other figures like a 'Rival Poet' who appears at one stage to have supplanted the poet in his patron-Friend's affections. The Friend is often identified with a 'M[aste]r W.H.', said in the publisher's dedication to be the 'only begetter' of the Sonnets; hence cases have been made out for William Herbert, Earl of Pembroke, or (reversing the initials) Henry Wriothesley, Earl of Southampton. But most scholars have mercifully turned from such detective-work to a study of the Sonnets as poetry.

The Sonnets afford a remarkable fusion of intensely human emotions with philosophic power. Their two leading motifs illustrate the combination. One is the uncertain relation between Poet and Friend, dogged by infidelities on both sides, by their common love of the Dark Lady, and by the Friend's fascination with the Rival Poet. But through these turns and torments, there seems to evolve a firm mutual love, ultimately perceived as a lasting universal force.

This marks the culmination of the other great theme of the Sonnets, the attack of time on beauty, youth and love. In the early 'Marriage Sonnets', the Poet exhorts his Friend to marry and have children who will inherit and thus preserve his graces. This somewhat crude solution soon yields to the promise of immortality through the Poet's own deathless verses. And gradually, even this is supplanted by the sense of love itself as a lasting relationship and eternal force.

These themes are not developed as consistently or sequentially as one would wish. Shakespeare seems to have written his Sonnets in the 1590s; but they were printed only in 1609 by Thomas Thorpe, a publisher of doubtful credentials, and may be neither complete nor correctly arranged. Efforts at rearranging them have also misfired. We must be content with glimpses of the 'inner story', and with remarkably intense treatments of complex themes in the brief compass of single poems or a linked group. The Sonnets are among the most tantalizing, most compelling poems in the English language.]

29 Sonnet 5: 'Those hours that with gentle work'

[One of the subtlest and most powerful of the 'Marriage Sonnets', where the poet presses his friend to 'preserve' his beauty in his children through marriage and procreation.]

Those hours that with gentle work did frame
The lovely gaze where every eye doth dwell
Will play the tyrants to the very same,
And that unfair which fairly doth excel;
For never-resting time leads summer on
To hideous winter and confounds him there,
Sap check'd with frost and lusty leaves quite gone,
Beauty o'ersnow'd and bareness everywhere.
Then were not summer's distillation left
A liquid prisoner pent in walls of glass,
Beauty's effect with beauty were bereft,
Nor it nor no remembrance what it was.
    But flowers distill'd, though they with winter meet,
    Leese but their show; their substance still lives sweet.

1 *Those hours* i.e., the passage of time. It is a common idea in the

Sonnets that time both nurtures and destroys youth and beauty. *gentle* (a) excellent, noble (b) kindly (cf. *tyrants*, l.3)

2 *lovely* (a) beautiful (b) lovable *gaze* something gazed at, a spectacle (OED 1)

4 *unfair* deprive of fairness or beauty; 'deface' (Rowse)
fairly beautifully, but also 'fully, truly' (OED 7). For the play on *fair*, cf. 30.7.

5 *leads on* suggests decoying or betraying

6 *confounds* ruins, destroys

7 *check'd* (its flow) stopped, obstructed *lusty* healthy, vigorous in growth (OED 5c)

8 *o'ersnowed* covered with snow

9 *summer's distillation* perfume distilled from summer flowers, compared to the Friend's beauty surviving in his children

10 *pent* imprisoned, contained *walls of glass* i.e., of the distilling vessel

11 'Beauty's impact would have been lost along with beauty itself.' *effect* result, influence, power

12 'Neither itself nor any memory of it'. The double negative (*nor . . . nor*) was a recognized Elizabethan device for emphasis.

14 *leese* lose *substance* essence *still* always

30 Sonnet 18: 'Shall I compare thee'

[The theme of 'immortality through verse' had been raised in a defeatist way in Sonnet 17. It is first given free expression in this poem.]

Shall I compare thee to a summer's day?
Thou art more lovely and more temperate.
Rough winds do shake the darling buds of May,
And summer's lease hath all too short a date.
Sometime too hot the eye of heaven shines,
And often is his gold complexion dimm'd;
And every fair from fair some time declines,
By chance or nature's changing course untrimm'd.
But thy eternal summer shall not fade,

Nor lose possession of that fair thou ow'st;
Nor shall death brag thou wand'rest in his shade,
When in eternal lines to time thou grow'st.
So long as men can breathe or eyes can see,
So long lives this, and this gives life to thee.

2 *temperate* moderate, mild, equable

3 *darling* beloved, favourite (of May or summer. In Elizabethan times, before the Gregorian reform of the calendar, May lasted almost till midsummer.)

4 *lease . . . date* the legal image of a short-term contract *date* duration

5 *eye of heaven* sun

7 'Every fair object falls off from its beauty at some time.' *declines* suggests the sunset (cf. ll.5-6).

8 *untrimm'd* deprived of 'trimness', elegance or beauty

10 *lose possession* cf. *lease*, l.4. The Friend does not have his beauty on lease; he owns it. *fair* fairness, beauty (like the second *fair*, l.7) *ow'st* own *possession . . . ow'st* draws out the legal image of l.4.

11 *his shade* In Hebrew, the shadow of death means intense darkness, but in English it is directly associated with death. Cf.Psalms 23:4: 'though I walk through the valley of the shadow of death.'

12 *to time* for all time, eternally (OED 45a). But *to time thou grow'st* may also = 'merge with, or become part of, time itself', like a graft to a tree.

31 Sonnet 29: 'When in disgrace with Fortune'

When in disgrace with Fortune and men's eyes,
I all alone beweep my outcast state,
And trouble deaf heaven with my bootless cries,
And look upon myself, and curse my fate,
Wishing me like to one more rich in hope,
Featur'd like him, like him with friends possess'd,
Desiring this man's art and that man's scope,

With what I most enjoy contented least;
Yet in these thoughts myself almost despising,
Haply I think on thee: and then my state,
Like to the lark at break of day arising
From sullen earth, sings hymns at heaven's gate.
    For thy sweet love remember'd, such wealth brings,
    That then I scorn to change my state with kings.

1 'When out of favour with Fortune and despised by men'
3 *bootless* unavailing, useless
5 *Wishing me like to* wishing I were like *rich in hope* (a) with rich hopes for the future (b) with better hope of wealth (Booth)
6 *Featur'd* looking *him . . . him* i.e., this man or that
7 *art* skill, learning *scope* 'reach or range of mental activity' (OED 6, first cited from this line)
8 (a) 'discontented with the greatest blessings I possess' (b) 'discontented with what I normally most enjoy'
10 *haply* by chance *state* mental state, mood (OED 2)
12 *sullen* gloomy, dismal (OED 3): first so used by Shakespeare *sings . . . gate* i.e., thanks and praises God
13 *wealth* not merely 'riches', but the basic sense of 'well-being' or 'happiness' (OED 1)
13–14 Leishman (pp. 202 ff.) says that this idea, that the poet's love compensates for all other misfortunes, has no real precedent in love-poetry.

32 Sonnet 54: 'O how much more doth beauty'

[A curious balance of themes brought out separately elsewhere. The Friend's beauty is no longer a sufficient praise; his 'truth' or virtue must validate it. But even this is preserved not by its own power but by the Poet's skill. There is also the disquieting undernote that, though the Friend is explicitly compared to the 'sweet roses', he affords comparison with the 'canker blooms' as well.]

O how much more doth beauty beauteous seem
By that sweet ornament which truth doth give!

The rose looks fair, but fairer we it deem
For that sweet odour which doth in it live.
The canker blooms have full as deep a dye
As the perfumed tincture of the roses,
Hang on such thorns, and play as wantonly
When summer's breath their masked buds discloses;
But for their virtue only is their show,
They live unwoo'd, and unrespected fade,
Die to themselves. Sweet roses do not so;
Of their sweet deaths are sweetest odours made.
        And so of you, beauteous and lovely youth,
        When that shall vade, by verse distils your truth.

2 *truth* (a) faith in love (b) truth of nature, virtue. Often taken only in the first sense, but surely implies the other.
5 *canker* wild rose or dog rose, which lacks scent; but suggests 'cankered', worm-eaten. *dye* i.e., colour
6 *tincture* colour *roses* i.e., cultivated roses
7 *such* similar *wantonly* playfully (OED b)
8 *masked* i.e., closed, concealed
9 i.e., Their only virtue is in their show.
10 *unwoo'd* unsought; but suggests women without lovers *unrespected* unregarded, neglected
11 *to themselves* i.e., lonely or unattended; also 'without profit to others' (Pooler) *sweet* i.e., sweet-smelling
13 *lovely* lovable
14 *vade* Then a common variant of *fade*, but suggesting decaying or perishing in particular. *by verse* Emended by Malone to 'my verse'. This is unnecessary if we take *distils* as intransitive: 'is distilled', 'distils out'. The reference is to extracting perfumes from flowers by distillation. Cf. 29 above.

33 Sonnet 55: 'Not marble, nor the gilded monuments'

[Echoes the close of Ovid's *Metamorphoses* (XV.871–9) and Horace, *Odes* III.xxx. But those poets speak of their own immortality through verse; Shakespeare, his Friend's. And the profound evocation of transience, violence and ruin is all Shakespeare's own.]

Not marble, nor the gilded monuments
Of princes, shall outlive this powerful rhyme:
But you shall shine more bright in these contents
Than unswept stone, besmear'd with sluttish time.
When wasteful war shall statues overturn
And broils root out the work of masonry,
Nor Mars his sword, nor war's quick fire shall burn
The living record of your memory.
'Gainst death and all-oblivious enmity
Shall you pace forth; your praise shall still find room
Even in the eyes of all posterity
That wear this world out to the ending doom.
So, till the judgment that yourself arise,
You live in this, and dwell in lovers' eyes.

3 *contents* of the book: these verses

4 *stone* i.e., a tombstone or memorial—now *unswept,* neglected and ill-maintained
besmear'd stained, hence sullied, defiled (OED 2)

5 *wasteful* destructive (OED 1), but implying 'futile, unprofitable'

6 *broils* wars, battles; but the word (properly 'tumults, quarrels') is contemptuous and reductive. Cf. *sluttish time* (l.4).
root out uproot, destroy *masonry* the mason's art or skill, rather than (as commonly) his work itself

7 *Mars his* Mars's: a common Renaissance variant for the possessive *quick* vigorous, strong (OED 11)
burn either = destroy, by any means (a rare use: OED 13d); or, more likely, referring to 'fire' alone by a loose zeugmatic construction

9 *all-oblivious* either (a) ignoring (oblivious of) all your virtues, or (b) inducing oblivion, erasing from human memory
enmity either of time or of human opponents

11–12 *all . . . doom* all successive generations till the end of the world (Doomsday or the Last Judgment)

13 *yourself arise* as all bodies will, from their graves, at the Last Judgment

14 *this* i.e., the verse *in lovers' eyes* either because lovers will read the verse; or, more interestingly, because lovers will see the Friend's ideal form reflected in their own beloved.

34 Sonnet 64: 'When I have seen'

[This and the next sonnet are perhaps Shakespeare's most powerful laments for the ravages of time. They may be companion pieces, and the theme of 'immortality through verse' concluding the second poem be applicable to both. But it is raised in a subdued, tentative spirit; and the despairing end of Sonnet 64 remains permanently valid.]

When I have seen by Time's fell hand defac'd
The rich proud cost of outworn buried age,
When sometime lofty towers I see down-raz'd,
And brass eternal slave to mortal rage;
When I have seen the hungry ocean gain
Advantage on the kingdom of the shore,
And the firm soil win of the watery main,
Increasing store with loss, and loss with store;
When I have seen such interchange of state,
Or state itself confounded to decay,
Ruin hath taught me thus to ruminate,
That Time will come and take my love away.
This thought is as a death, which cannot choose
But weep to have that which it fears to lose.

1 *fell* cruel, destructive

2 Finely blends the *idea* of time and change with the concrete, visual image of old buildings and ruins. *cost* any costly object: wealth, pomp, splendour *outworn buried age* i.e., old kings, empires, societies etc.—buried in the grave, or as ruins under ground.

3 *sometime* once, erstwhile *down-raz'd* razed to the ground

4 *brass eternal* Horace called his verse *aere perennius*, 'more lasting than bronze' (*Odes* III.xxx.1) *mortal* death-dealing.

Note the antithesis of *eternal . . . mortal* *rage* either literally (war or violence), or generally of the destructive force of time

5–8 Nature and the way elements suffer change and destruction. Echoes Ovid, *Metamorphoses* XV. 261 ff.

5–6 *gain advantage* win, as in a battle or invasion

7 *main* the open sea

8 i.e., One side's store (accumulation or increase) is the other's loss.

9 *interchange of state* Cf. 'exchanged their estate' in Arthur Golding's 1567 translation of Ovid's *Metamorphoses* XV. 287.

9–10 A progressive exploration of the word *state* from 'political state or empire' to 'condition', 'state of existence' (as land, sea etc.) and finally in l.10 to 'existence' itself.

11 Expressive alliteration in *r* and, supporting it, in *m/n*. The long echoing *ruminate* is followed up by the monosyllabic simplicity of l.12. *ruin* the process, but suggests the actual physical ruins of buildings etc.

13 *as a death* i.e., as disquieting as the beloved's death itself

35 Sonnet 65: 'Since brass, nor stone'

Since brass, nor stone, nor earth, nor boundless sea
But sad mortality o'ersways their power,
How with this rage shall beauty hold a plea,
Whose action is no stronger than a flower?
O how shall summer's honey breath hold out
Against the wrackful siege of battering days,
When rocks impregnable are not so stout,
Nor gates of steel so strong, but time decays?
O fearful meditation! Where, alack,
Such Time's best jewel from Time's chest lie hid?
Or what strong hand can hold his swift foot back?
Or who his spoil of beauty can forbid?
    O none, unless this miracle have might,
    That in black ink my love may still shine bright.

1 *Since* elliptical: 'Since there is neither . . .'

2 *sad* calamitous, inflicting sorrow (OED 5f) *mortality* death *o'ersways* overrules

3 *rage* violence, fury—perhaps madness (OED 4.1). Cf. **34**.4.

4 *action* power, efficacy; but *plea* . . . *action* suggests a legal metaphor. *flower* proverbially short-lived. The poem exploits the antithesis of soft and hard: flowers against brass and stone, 'honey breath' against 'battering days' (ll.5, 6)

5 *honey breath* sweet breath: suggests the summer breeze, also bees gathering honey from summer flowers

6 *wrackful* destructive *battering* The gates of a besieged town would be broken down with a battering-ram.

7,8 *rocks, gates of steel* usual defences in a siege *decays* with 'them' as object understood

10 *Time's best jewel* i.e., the Friend. Implies that Time, having created the Friend's beauty, will seize him for his own treasury (*chest*). Shakespeare constantly suggests that time both creates and destroys beauty: cf. Sonnets 60.8, 73.12. For the chest and jewel imagery, cf. Sonnets 48, 52.

12 *spoil* (a)'spoils', loot, plunder (b) 'spoiling', damage, destruction

13 *might* power, efficacy

13–14 Cf Sonnet 63.13-14. What was there a certainty is here merely a hope.

36 Sonnet 73: 'That time of year'

[Powerfully dramatic, even tragic theme of a love growing rather than declining with the lover's old age and imminent death. (Shakespeare himself could scarcely have been so old when he wrote the poem.) The sonnet also shows perfect formal integration of the English sonnet-scheme: the three quatrains build up an idea through three distinct images, with an arresting reversal in the couplet.]

That time of year thou may'st in me behold
When yellow leaves, or none, or few, do hang
Upon those boughs which shake against the cold,
Bare, ruin'd choirs, where late the sweet birds sang.
In me thou seest the twilight of such day

As after sunset fadeth in the west,
Which by and by black night doth take away,
Death's second self, that seals up all in rest.
In me thou seest the glowing of such fire
That on the ashes of his youth doth lie,
As the death-bed whereon it must expire,
Consum'd with that which it was nourish'd by.
This thou perceiv'st, which makes thy love more strong,
To love that well, which thou must leave ere long.

2 *or . . . or* Old form of *either . . . or*

3 Implicit image of an old man's trembling body. A very complex image-cluster in this quatrain: old age compared to winter, and wintry trees to ruined choirs as well as aged bodies. *cold* cold wind

4 *choirs* choir-stalls. To the Elizabethan reader, would suggest the ruined chapels and abbeys (many still standing today) left by the dissolution of the monasteries after the Protestant Reformation. *birds* compared, by implication, to the choristers

5–6 *such . . . west* Syntax unclear. Either 'the day at such a state or point as after sunset . . . ', or 'such portion of daylight as remains after sunset and fades . . . '

8 *second self* another form or image. The night is conventionally an image or reminder of death.
Note the alliteration in *s* in this line.

10 *his* till *c.* 1600, the common possessive form of *it*; but here, probably indicates personification of the fire *his youth* i.e., its early stages, when it had enough fuel

12 *with* (a) by: the fuel, now turned to ashes, is smothering the fire (b) along with, together with
that i.e., the fuel. A common idea in Shakespeare's Sonnets: the natural force which first fosters life later destroys it.

37 Sonnet 78: 'So oft have I invok'd thee'

[One of the first sonnets where the poet talks resentfully of a 'Rival Poet' to whom the Friend has shown favour. As yet, however, the direct reference is to rivals generally and not a particular one. Makes the conventional point that convention is artificial, while this poet speaks plainly and sincerely.]

So oft have I invok'd thee for my muse,
And found such fair assistance in my verse,
As every alien pen hath got my use,
And under thee their poesy disperse.
Thine eyes, that taught the dumb on high to sing
And heavy ignorance aloft to fly,
Have added feathers to the learned's wing,
And given grace a double majesty.
Yet be most proud of that which I compile,
Whose influence is thine, and born of thee:
In other's works thou dost but mend the style,
And arts with thy sweet graces graced be.
    But thou art all my art, and dost advance
    As high as learning, my rude ignorance.

1 *invok'd . . . muse* made you the subject (hence inspiration) for my poetry

2 *fair assistance* favourable support: perhaps patronage, but more likely inspiration

3 *As* that *alien* i.e., other's *got my use* either (a) followed my practice (of praising you) or (b) imitated my style

4 *under thee* i.e., under either your inspiration or your patronage. *Under* was speciallyusedinfluence of heavenly bodies (OED 1): cf. 1.1n. *disperse* circulate

5 *on high* aloud (OED *high* 18b); but suggests a flying, singing bird (cf. ll.6-7), perhaps Shakespeare's favourite lark (see 31.11).

5–8 'Your beauty has inspired even the unskilful and ignorant, and doubly endowed the learned and skilful.'

9 *compile* compose (OED 3)

10 *influence* an astrological term: the power of stars etc.

11–14 Follows from ll.5–8. 'Skilful poets only gain some extra advantage when they write about you; but to me, otherwise incapable, you are the only source of inspiration, which is of more credit to you. You merely enhance their rhetoric, but provide all the substance of my verse.'

13 *advance* raise

38 Sonnet 97: 'How like a winter'

[Another version of the common idea that love can defeat time. Here it counters the cycle of the seasons, in one of the most powerful extended conceits anywhere in the Sonnets.]

How like a winter hath my absence been
From thee, the pleasure of the fleeting year!
What freezings have I felt, what dark days seen,
What old December's bareness everywhere!
And yet this time remov'd was summer's time:
The teeming autumn, big with rich increase,
Bearing the wanton burden of the prime
Like widow'd wombs after their lords' decease.
Yet this abundant issue seem'd to me
But hope of orphans and unfather'd fruit,
For summer and his pleasures wait on thee,
And thou away, the very birds are mute.
  Or if they sing, 'tis with so dull a cheer
  That leaves look pale, dreading the winter's near.

2 *pleasure* source of joy *pleasure of the year* i.e., spring
5 *time remov'd* the time that I was removed or absent from you
5–6 The context makes *summer* and *autumn* interchangeable: autumn's fruits are still in the womb.
6–10 The fruits of autumn are seen as posthumous children, growing physically but with no hope of security or prosperity.
6 *teeming* pregnant, fecund (OED 1) *increase* growth, of crops or offspring
7 *wanton* profuse, luxuriant (OED 7); but also lascivious, unchaste *prime* spring, when this growth was generated or conceived; but also youth, thus (with *wanton*) implying the unwanted offspring (*burden*) of a brief youthful dalliance
9 *issue* offspring (OED 6); but also 'produce, profits' (OED 7)—hence *fruit*, l.10. The produce or wealth of autumn seemed no more than the meagre prospects (*hope*) of orphans.
10 *unfather'd* fatherless
13 *cheer* mood, disposition (OED 3)

39 Sonnet 110: 'Alas, 'tis true'

[Interesting in that Shakespeare's lament for a futile life seems to allude to the frustrations of the actor-playwright's pursuit, producing mere displays and shadows of truth.]

Alas, 'tis true I have gone here and there
And made myself a motley to the view,
Gor'd mine own thoughts, sold cheap what is most dear,
Made old offences of affections new.
Most true it is, that I have look'd on truth
Askance and strangely; but by all above,
These blenches gave my heart another youth,
And worse essays prov'd thee my best of love.
Now all is done, have what shall have no end:
Mine appetite I never more will grind
On newer proof, to try an older friend,
A god in love, to whom I am confin'd.
    Then give me welcome, next my heaven the best,
    Even to thy pure and most most loving breast.

2 *a motley* a jester or clown, from the motley (particoloured costume) he wore. Suggests 'a diversity of interests and guises, and may cover social activity as well as stage composition and stage performances' (Wilson Knight).

3 *gor'd* stabbed, wounded; perhaps also 'sullied, befouled' (*gore*=dirt, filth: OED 1) *dear* (a) costly; (b) beloved

3-4 Refers at one level to his cheapening his love through public expression in the Sonnets; more deeply (cf. ll.9-11) to deserting his true love for his Friend for baser and less lasting affections (probably for the Dark Lady). But also refers obliquely, like ll.5-6, to the inadequacies of dramatic form and public performance.

5 *truth* loyalty in love; but surely 'truth' in the full philosophical sense as well. Note the play on *true . . . truth*.

6 *strangely* like a stranger: coldly, distantly (OED 1)
all above all the heavens or gods

7 *blenches* side-glances (OED 2, from this line only); hence 'swervings, inconstancy' (Onions, *Shakespeare Glossary*)

another youth i.e., renewed love (for the Friend)
8 *essays* trials, tests, experiments (OED 1)
prov'd . . . love (a) proved you to be my best beloved; (b) gave you proof of my best love
10-11 'I will not again put my love (*appetite*) for you, my old friend, to the test (*proof*) afforded by new passing loves.'
grind (a) whet, sharpen, restrengthen; (b) afflict, torment (OED 3) *try* (a) put (one's love) to test; (b) annoy, afflict
12 *a god in love* i.e., an ideal lover; also suggests the god of love or Cupid *confin'd* restricted, bound (by fate or loyalty)
13 *next . . . best* my greatest blessing next to heaven or salvation
14 *most most* repeated for emphasis

40 Sonnet 116: 'Let me not to the marriage'

[This celebration of an ideal, eternal love is triumphantly clear; less so the situation hinted at in ll.1–4. It seems the Poet agrees to let his Friend seek a 'marriage of true minds' elsewhere; his own love for the Friend will not change.

The language recalls 1 Corinthians 13: amorous love passes into the Christian love or charity enjoined by St Paul.]

Let me not to the marriage of true minds
Admit impediments: love is not love
Which alters when it alteration finds,
Or bends with the remover to remove.
O no, it is an ever-fixed mark
That looks on tempests and is never shaken;
It is the star to every wand'ring bark,
Whose worth's unknown, although his height be taken.
Love's not Time's fool, though rosy lips and cheeks
Within his bending sickle's compass come;
Love alters not with his brief hours and weeks,
But bears it out even to the edge of doom.
    If this be error, and upon me prov'd,
    I never writ, nor no man ever lov'd.

1–2 Echoes the Anglican marriage service, where the priest asks the assembly whether there is any 'impediment' (e.g., a previous alliance) to the marriage. The Poet will not impede his Friend's new love by advancing their own earlier relationship.

4 *bendes . . . remove* changes course, to shift or disappear, when its object does

5 From this point, 'love' becomes more and more an abstract, super-human force rather than a private relationship. Thus Shakespeare can reverse the Petrarchan image of the storm-tossed or shipwrecked lover (see headnote to **4**): love is the pole star, never 'shaken' though particular lovers may not perceive it.
mark sea-mark, beacon; but *ever-fixed* suggests the pole star as in l.7.

7 *wand'ring* strayed, off-course *bark* ship

8 'We know its nature or object, but not its full power'
worth astrological power or influence *height* altitude, degree of elevation *taken* measured (OED 32b)

9 *fool* dupe, victim

10 *bending* bent, like the sickle; but suggests how age bends or bows the body. *sickle* the traditional attribute of 'Time the Mower', as 'All flesh is grass' (Isaiah 40:6). But direct reference to 'rosy lips and cheeks' makes Time's action specially savage.

11 *his* i.e., Time's

12 *bears it out* endures (OED 15b) *edge of doom* verge of Doomsday, end of the world

13 *upon me* against me, to my charge

41 Sonnet 125: 'Were't aught to me'

[Allied to Sonnet 116, but with more sense of an intimate personal love. The poet rebuts slanderers who say that he does not pay due honour to his noble Friend, or does so only for gain or favour.]

Were't aught to me I bore the canopy,
With my extern the outward honouring,
Or laid great bases for eternity,

Which proves more short than waste or ruining?
Have I not seen dwellers on form and favour
Lose all and more by paying too much rent,
For compound sweet forgoing simple savour—
Pitiful thrivers, in their gazing spent?
No, let me be obsequious in thy heart,
And take thou my oblation, poor but free,
Which is not mix'd with seconds, knows no art
But mutual render, only me for thee.
    Hence, thou suborn'd informer! A true soul,
    When most impeach'd, stands least in thy control.

1 *Were't . . . bore* Would it matter to me, or profit me, if I bore
canopy as a sign of pomp or rank

2 *extern* externals, body and actions *the outward* the Friend's physical beauty, or his rank and public image

3 *laid . . . eternity* prepared to ensure your eternal honour and fame. Image of the foundations of palaces etc.

4 *which* the desired eternity, which proves more short-lived than destruction itself (*waste or ruining*)

5 *dwellers on* people 'dwelling on' or absorbed with
form and favour (a) form and face, external beauty (b) rank and favour or benefits received

6 *rent* i.e., service or attentions, as 'payment' for favours: suggested by *dwellers* (l.5)

7 'Forgoing simple pleasures for impure or complex ones.' *Compound* is probably the adjective and *sweet* (sweet substance, hence pleasure: OED 3) the noun. *savour* taste The image is of 'simple' nectars or essences (unmixed, distilled from a single plant) against mixed ones.

8 *pitiful thrivers* i.e., thriving yet pitiable men; or perhaps those thriving pitifully, i.e., not thriving at all *in . . . spent* exhausted merely by looking on hopefully

9 *obsequious* obedient, devoted: no pejorative suggestion
in thy heart i.e., not in external show

10 *oblation* offering (originally religious sense) *free* freely given, without ulterior motive

11 *seconds* inferior substances: alloys, adulterants
art artifice, deception

12 *mutual render* i.e., surrendering or offering each to the other

13 *suborn'd informer* bribed or false witness: the type of slanderer the poet is condemning

14 *impeach'd* accused, disparaged

42 Sonnet 130: 'My mistress' eyes'

[This and the remaining Sonnets are from the 'Dark Lady' sequence, where Shakespeare often works a vein of shock and paradox. The Lady is not conventionally beautiful; their love is worldly-wise and mutually unfaithful, yet mature, fulfilling and stimulating.

Here the mistress is opposed in all respects to the standard poetic images of beauty: eyes like the sun, lips like coral, breasts white as snow, hair like gold wires, rosy cheeks, perfumed breath, a voice like music. The poet's love thus appears as a simple sincere emotion, unadorned truth. (This is itself a conventional notion.) The mistress is not really ugly: indeed, she may be as pretty as any other woman (see ll.13–14). It is simply that she must be praised in terms more authentic than the conventional. The final lines are a pointed overthrow of Petrarchan sentiment.]

My mistress' eyes are nothing like the sun;
Coral is far more red than her lips' red;
If snow be white, why then her breasts are dun;
If hairs be wires, black wires grow on her head.
I have seen roses damask'd, red and white,
But no such roses see I in her cheeks;
And in some perfumes is there more delight
Than in the breath that from my mistress reeks.
I love to hear her speak, yet well I know
That music hath a far more pleasing sound.
I grant I never saw a goddess go:
My mistress, when she walks, treads on the ground.
    And yet by heaven, I think my love as rare
    As any she belied with false compare.

4 Black hair was then unfashionable. The 'darkness' of the Lady

is a matter of hair and eyes as much as complexion.

5 *damask'd* pink or blush red (mixed *red and white*): the original colour of the *damask* or Damascene rose

8 *reeks* Could be used of any scent, even perfume; but was already applied chiefly to unpleasant smells.

14 *any she* any woman *belied* misrepresented, falsely lauded *false compare* false comparisons (like those mocked above); but also *false* = insincere, flattering

43 Sonnet 144: 'Two loves I have'

[The classic expression of the Poet's two opposed loves, for the Friend and the Dark Lady; and more fundamentally, for two opposed tendencies in all human love, spiritual and physical, elevating and corrupting, reflecting the duality of human nature itself. This is presented here as the battle of good and evil angels for a man's soul: a familiar motif in medieval art and literature, including the morality play, of which Shakespeare might have seen some of the last performances, and which certainly influenced his work.]

Two loves I have, of comfort and despair,
Which like two spirits do suggest me still:
The better angel is a man right fair,
The worser spirit a woman colour'd ill.
To win me soon to hell, my female evil
Tempteth my better angel from my side,
And would corrupt my saint to be a devil,
Wooing his purity with her foul pride.
And whether that my angel be turned fiend,
Suspect I may, yet not directly tell;
But being both from me, both to each friend,
I guess one angel in another's hell.
    Yet this shall I ne'er know, but live in doubt
    Till my bad angel fire my good one out.

1 *Two loves* i.e., the Friend and the Dark Lady

2 *spirits* supernatural beings, angels *suggest* urge, prompt

(especially to evil: OED 2) *still* always

4 *colour'd ill* i.e., dark

5 *hell* of torment and jealousy as the Lady seduces the Friend (ll.5–12): the Poet is concerned at this double betrayal of his love. The situation is reflected in Sonnets 33–35, 40–42, 133–34.

8 *pride* the cardinal sin; but also 'finery, display' (OED 6, 7), making an oxymoron with *foul*. Further, *pride* = sexual urge, especially 'heat' in female animals (OED 11).

10 *directly* plainly, exactly

11 *from me* away or parted from me *both to each friend* friends to each other

12 *one . . . hell* i.e., The Lady has corrupted the Friend.

13 *doubt* fear (OED 3) as well as 'uncertainty, suspense'

14 *fire . . . out* usually 'drive out by fire' (OED 8), but here perhaps 'burn out, destroy completely by fire' (cf. OED 2).

44 Sonnet 147: 'My love is as a fever'

[One of Shakespeare's strongest indictments of the destructive power of love. Cf. Sonnet 129.]

My love is as a fever, longing still
For that which longer nurseth the disease,
Feeding on that which doth preserve the ill,
Th'uncertain sickly appetite to please.
My reason, the physician to my love,
Angry that his prescriptions are not kept,
Hath left me, and I, desperate, now approve
Desire is death, which physic did except.
Past cure I am, now reason is past care,
And frantic-mad with evermore unrest;
My thoughts and my discourse as madmen's are,
At random from the truth vainly express'd.
    For I have sworn thee fair, and thought thee bright,
    Who art as black as hell, as dark as night.

1 *still* always 1, 2 play on *longing, longer*

2 *nurseth* i.e., preserves, sustains

3 *ill* illness, disease (OED 6)

5 Love was traditionally viewed as a 'passion' overpowering the 'reason' that should govern it.

6 *prescriptions* any orders or instructions, not only for medicines (Ingram & Redpath)

7 *desperate* incurable (OED 3) *approve* prove true, demonstrate

8 'Love or passion (*desire*) which has refused medicine (*physic*) means (i.e., leads to) death.'
except object to, refuse (peculiarly Shakespearean: OED 4)

9 *past care* past caring, having given up responsibility

10 *frantic-mad* raving mad, violently mad *evermore* a very unusual adjectival use

12 *at random* haphazardly *from* away from, diverging from
vainly (a) uselessly, futilely; (b) foolishly, meaninglessly

14 *black as hell* The Lady's appearance becomes metaphorical. Cf. Sonnet 144 and, for the reversal of common perception through love, Sonnets 137, 148, 150.

Christopher Marlowe

45 : The Passionate Shepherd To His Love

[Published in this six-stanza form, under this title, in the famous collection of pastoral poems, *England's Helicon* (1600). Stanzas 1, 2, 3 and 5 had appeared in a 1599 collection, *The Passionate Pilgrim*. The other two stanzas—which alone have a pastoral content—may be the *Helicon* editor's addition.]

Come live with me and be my love,
And we will all the pleasures prove
That valleys, groves, hills and fields,
Woods, or steepy mountain yields.

And we will sit upon the rocks,
Seeing the shepherds feed their flocks
By shallow rivers, to whose falls
Melodious birds sing madrigals.

And I will make thee beds of roses,
And a thousand fragrant posies,
A cap of flowers, and a kirtle
Embroider'd all with leaves of myrtle;

A gown made of the finest wool
Which from our pretty lambs we pull;
Fair-lined slippers for the cold,
With buckles of the purest gold;

A belt of straw and ivy-buds,
With coral clasps and amber studs:
And if these pleasures may thee move,
Come live with me and be my love.

The shepherd-swains shall dance and sing
For thy delight each May morning:
If these delights thy mind may move,
Then live with me, and be my love.

2 *prove* try, experience

3 The smoother and better-known version of this line in *The Passionate Pilgrim* reads 'That hills and valleys, dales and fields'.

4 *steepy* Elizabethan variant of *steep*

7 *shallow* hence murmuring more loudly *to whose falls* to (the sound of) its cascades or waterfalls

8 *madrigals* love-songs; particularly 'part-songs' blending several voices

11 *kirtle* gown (OED 2)

12 *with . . . myrtle* i.e., with a myrtle-leaf design

19 *And if* for 'an if', a stock phrase (*an* = if)

22 *May morning* May-games were a shepherd's festival in fact and still more in pastoral convention.

Sir Walter Ralegh

46 : The Nymph's Reply

This poem was printed as 'Ignoto' (anonymous) in *England's Helicon* in 1600. (One stanza had appeared earlier in *The Passionate Pilgrim.*) In Izaak Walton's book on fishing, *The Complete Angler* 1653), it is ascribed to Ralegh. There, a young milkmaid sings Marlowe's poem and her mother returns this as an 'answer'.]

If all the world and love were young,
And truth in every shepherd's tongue,
These pretty pleasures might me move
To live with thee and be thy love.

But time drives flocks from field to fold
When rivers rage and rocks grow cold,
And Philomel becometh dumb;
The rest complains of cares to come.

The flowers do fade, and wanton fields
To wayward Winter reckoning yields:
A honey tongue, a heart of gall
Is fancy's spring, but sorrow's fall.

Thy gowns, thy shoes, thy beds of roses,
Thy cap, thy kirtle, and thy posies,
Soon break, soon wither—soon forgotten,
In folly ripe, in reason rotten.

Thy belt of straw and ivy-buds,
Thy coral clasps and amber studs,
All these in me no means can move
To come to thee and be thy love.

But could youth last, and love still breed,
Had joys no date nor age no need,
Then these delights my mind might move
To live with thee and be thy love.

Nymph simply 'maiden' or 'girl', as often in Elizabethan poetry

1 *world* life, human existence (the earliest meaning)

5 *from field to fold* from summer to winter quarters. ll.5–12 are seasonal imagery for time and age.

7 *Philomel* the nightingale. Philomela, daughter of King Pandion, turned to a nightingale after her brother-in-law Tereus ravished her.

8 *the rest* i.e., the other birds—which go on singing, but only to lament their *cares* or sufferings in the winter *to come*

9 *wanton* lush, luxuriant (OED 7); but also 'lustful, unchaste', hence meeting its *reckoning* (l.10) in the winter of old age

10 *wayward* untoward (OED 1b), hostile, harsh; but also 'unruly, uncontrolled', lustfully despoiling' (*wanton*: l.9) spring. Ll.9–10 image the fate of wanton women, which this nymph wishes to avoid.

11 *gall* bile, bitterness. The lover's sweet tongue induces a springtime of *fancy* (light love: cf. Shakespeare, *The Merchant of Venice* III.ii.67–9), but leads to a *fall* or autumn of sorrow.

13–20 Cf. 45.9–20.

14 *posies* spelt *poesies* in the original, suggesting love-verses as well as posies of flowers

21 *still* for ever *breed* grow, increase

22 *date* limit, end (OED 5) *nor . . . need* if there were no need (necessity, compulsion) to age

Thomas Lodge

47 : 'Love guards the roses'

[From *Phillis* (1593), a pastoralized sequence of sonnets and other poems.]

Love guards the roses of thy lips
    And flies about them like a bee;
If I approach he forward skips,
    And if I kiss he stingeth me.

Love in thine eyes doth build his bower
    And sleeps within their pretty shine;
And if I look the boy will lour
    And from their orbs shoot shafts divine.

Love works thy heart within his fire
    And in my tears doth firm the same;
And if I tempt it will retire,
    And of my plaints doth make a game.

Love, let me cull her choicest flowers;
    And pity me, and calm her eye;
Make soft her heart, dissolve her lours:
    Then will I praise thy deity.

But if thou do not, Love, I'll truly serve her
In spite of thee, and by firm faith deserve her.

1 *Love* Cupid (see 1.7) *guards* Bullen's 1891 emendation of the original *guides*

1–2 Cf. a song in Lodge's romance *Rosalynde*: 'Love in my bosom like a bee/Doth suck his sweet.'

6 *shine* shining, radiance

8 *their orbs* i.e., the eyeballs
shaft divine the golden arrows that inspire love

9 'Love moulds or fashions your heart like metal melted over a fire.'

10 *tears* like the water used to cool molten iron
firm harden: Phillis has a hard heart

11 *tempt* attempt, try (to advance or approach)

13 The lover now addresses Love, so Phillis is no longer 'thou' but 'she'.

15 *lours* frowns. Applied to storm-clouds, hence *dissolve* (in rain—i.e., tears)

16 *deity* godhead, divinity

17–18 A twist in the tail. The lover defies the God of Love but not the mistress. Instead of threatening to reject the mistress, as 'But if thou do not . . .' might lead us to expect, he declares the Petrarchan intent of 'firm faith'.

Robert Southwell

48 : The Burning Babe

[One of the high points of the Elizabethan religious lyric, but written in conflict with the dominant current of the times. Southwell was a Catholic, a Jesuit priest who suffered imprisonment, torture and finally death for his religious work. His Catholic inheritance might explain the unusually clear echo, here in this poem, of the long medieval convention of addresses to the poet or other audience by Christ, the Virgin Mary etc. The 'Babe' is of course the infant Christ, born to save mankind by his death on the cross. But though this is obvious from the start to any Christian reader, the account of the vision in unspecified, immediate terms and the simulated 'discovery' of the truth in the last line lends the poem a suspense and vitality till the end.

The images and conceits of the poem anticipate Metaphysical poetry. The physical paradox of the Child 'burning' in the midst of snow is reinforced by others indicated in the notes. In ll.9–13 the fire becomes that of a forge or smithy fashioning men's souls; this turns into a 'bath' in l.14.]

As I in hoary winter's night stood shivering in the snow,
Surpris'd I was with sudden heat, which made my heart to glow:
And lifting up a fearful eye to view what fire was near,
A pretty babe all burning bright did in the air appear
Who, scorched with excessive heat, such floods of tears did shed,
As though his floods should quench his flames, which with his tears were bred.
'Alas,' quoth he, 'but newly born, in fiery heats I fry,
Yet none approach to warm their hearts, or feel my fire but I.

My faultless breast the furnace is; the fuel, wounding thorns;
Love is the fire, and sighs the smoke; the ashes, shames and scorns.
The fuel Justice layeth on, and Mercy blows the coals;
The metal in this furnace wrought are men's defiled souls:
For which, as now on fire I am to work them to their good,
So will I melt into a bath, to wash them in my blood.'
With this he vanish'd out of sight, and swiftly shrunk away,
And straight I called unto mind that it was Christmas day.

1 *hoary* white—i.e., snowy
2 *heart to glow* both literally and metaphorically
3 *fearful* full of fear
5 *scorched . . . floods* This paradox is a reworking of the conventional state of the Petrarchan lover, like 'burning in ice'. It was common to rework Petrarchan love-conventions to religious use—as later, for instance, in George Herbert.
7 *fry* burn
9 *faultless* free from sin *thorns* with which Christ was crowned during his Passion
10 *shames and scorns* heaped on Christ during his Passion. Note how, by a continual paradox, Christ's pain and suffering become inseparable from his love. Similarly, Justice demands that he must die as ransom for man's sin, but Mercy impels him to offer himself (l.11).
11 *blows the coals* fans the fire
12 *men's defiled souls* which Christ is redeeming from sin by his sacrifice
13 *work them* like metal being wrought
14 *melt* presumably with the heat

William Shakespeare

49 : 'On a day — alack the day!'

[A love-poem composed by Dumain, one of the courtiers in *Love's Labour's Lost* (IV.iii.98 ff.). Reprinted, slightly abridged, in *The Passionate Pilgrim* (1599) and, with a pastoral touch, in *England's Helicon* (1600). Cf. Richard Barnfield's 'As it fell upon a day' (also in *The Passionate Pilgrim*) and Nicholas Breton's 'In the merry month of May'. Both songs are to be found in *England's Helicon* and in Norman Ault's *Elizabethan Lyrics*.]

On a day—alack the day!
Love, whose month is every May,
Spied a blossom passing fair
Playing in the wanton air.
Through the velvet leaves the wind,
All unseen, 'gan passage find:
That the lover, sick to death,
Wish'd himself the heaven's breath.
'Air,' quoth he, 'thy cheeks may blow:
Air, would I might triumph so!
But alack! My hand is sworn
Ne'er to pluck thee from thy thorn:
Vow, alack, for youth unmeet,
Youth so apt to pluck a sweet.
Do not call it sin in me
That I am forsworn for thee:
Thou for whom Jove would swear
Juno but an Ethiop were,
And deny himself for Jove,
Turning mortal for thy love.

2 (a) 'Love, for whom May is always the appropriate month;

(b) 'Love, for whom it is always May or springtime'. *Love* may be Cupid, but is more likely the emotion itself.

3 *blossom* clearly standing for a girl. *Wanton* ('playful', but also 'flirtatious, 'light-of-love') suggests her ambience and her own spirit. *passing* surpassingly, supremely

5–8 The lover wishes that he, like the wind, could pass unseen through the leaves to caress the 'blossom'. *Pluck . . . thorn* (l.12) suggests further physical possession.

9 *thy . . . blow* Well may your cheeks blow (in view of such a target)

12 *thee, thy* refers to the 'blossom', but *thy* in l.9 to the air *thorn* i.e., the bush where 'the blossom' is growing. But obviously suggests a rose, the standard emblem of beauty or passion, with 'thorns' of another sort.

13 *unmeet* unfit

14 *sweet* sweet-smelling flower (cf. OED 7): more generally, any pleasure or delight

15–16 Refers to the dramatic situation of *Love's Labour's Lost*. Like his fellow-courtiers, Dumain has betrayed his vow of celibacy by falling in love (with Katherine, a French court lady, whom he addresses here).

17 *Jove* Jupiter. His divinely beautiful queen Juno would seem ugly beside the lover's mistress.

18 *Ethiop* Ethiopian: wrongly thought to be black-skinned and hence, in the customary European view, ugly

19 *deny . . . Jove* deny that he were Jove, instead putting on human form (*turning mortal*, l.20) to have access to the mistress

50 : 'O mistress mine'

[Sung by Feste the clown to Sir Toby Belch and Sir Andrew Aguecheek in *Twelfth Night* II.iii.40–53. The theme is the common one usually called, quoting Horace's classic phrase (*Odes* I.xi.8), *Carpe diem*, 'Pluck the day', like a flower that will soon fade: i.e., enjoy youth and love before you grow old and die. Such an invitation turns on a very fine balance between the opposite truths of love and death. In *Twelfth Night*, the audience of two old topers lends ironic poignancy to an apparently simple, cheerful rendering of the theme.

The song may have been sung to a tune entitled 'O mistress mine' in *The First Book of Consort Lessons* (1599) by the great Elizabethan musician Thomas Morley.]

O mistress mine, where are you roaming?
O stay and hear: your true love's coming,
    That can sing both high and low.
Trip no further, pretty sweeting:
Journeys end in lover's meeting,
    Every wise man's son doth know.

What is love? 'Tis not hereafter.
Present mirth hath present laughter,
    What's to come is still unsure.
In delay there lies no plenty.
Then come kiss me, sweet and twenty:
    Youth's a stuff will not endure.

4 *trip* go nimbly or lightly—as a graceful girl would
6 *wise man's son* Might mean just that; but a proverb says 'Wise men have foolish sons', and the singer here is a clown or fool.
7 *hereafter* i.e., a matter for the future
9 *still* always
10 *no plenty* no gain or advantage
11 *sweet and twenty* Apparently an Elizabethan idiom for 'pretty girl'—a sweet twenty-year-old. Might also imply twenty sweet kisses.
12 *stuff* cloth, material

Ben Jonson

51 : 'Come, my Celia'

[In the play *Volpone,* the lustful old trickster Volpone sings this song as he attempts to seduce the virtuous Celia, placed in Volpone's hands by her own husband in the hope of a legacy. The sordid context gives an ironic dimension to the delicately meditative lyricism of the opening, which closely imitates Catullus' Latin lyric *Vivamus, mea Lesbia, atque amemus* ('Let us live and love, my Lesbia'). This was one of the most famous classical poems on the theme of *Carpe diem* (see p. 119).

The latter part, original to Jonson, suggests a more mundane love-intrigue. However, Jonson incorporated the close of Catullus' poem in another lyric ('Kiss me, sweet'), showing his intimate absorption of classical models.]

Come, my Celia, let us prove
While we can, the sports of love.
Time will not be ours for ever:
He at length our good will sever.
Spend not then his gifts in vain:
Suns that set may rise again,
But if once we lose this light,
'Tis with us perpetual night.
Why should we defer our joys?
Fame and rumour are but toys.
Cannot we delude the eyes
Of a few poor household spies,
Or his easier ears beguile,
So removed by our wile?
'Tis no sin love's fruit to steal,
But the sweet theft to reveal:

To be taken, to be seen,
These have crimes accounted been.

1 *prove* try, taste
4 *good* pleasures, well-being *sever* cut off, remove, destroy
10 *fame* (a) report, rumour (b) reputation, hence fear of losing one's reputation. *rumour* gossip. Catullus exhorts Lesbia to dismiss 'the talk of crabbed old men', using the Latin word *rumor* ('reputation' as well as 'gossip' or 'hearsay'). *toys* trifles
12 *household spies* servants set to spy on their mistress's activities
13 *his* i.e., the husband's *easier* more easily deceived
14 'Whom we have cleverly got out of the way'
17 *taken* caught, found out

52 : On English Monsieur

[This is formally an epigram: a brief, compressed, usually witty poem, cultivated for both compliment and satire, on the two disparate models of the Greek Anthology and the Latin poet Martial. The satirical function links it to the wider currents of Renaissance satire, first notably cultivated in English by Wyatt and later by Donne, Hall, Marston, Wither etc., as also by Jonson in his comedies.

The Frenchified Englishman, like others affecting foreign garb and manners, was a stock object of satire. Fastidious Brisk in Jonson's play *Every Man out of His Humour* is a good instance.]

Would you believe, when you this Monsieur see,
That his whole body should speak French, not he?
That so much scarf of France, and hat, and feather,
And shoe, and tie, and garter should come hither
And land on one whose face durst never be
Toward the sea, farther than half-way tree?
That he, untravell'd, should be French so much,
As Frenchmen in his company should seem Dutch?
Or had his father, when he did him get,
The French disease, with which he labours yet,

Or hung some Monsieur's picture on the wall,
By which his dam conceiv'd him, clothes and all?
Or is it some French statue? No: 't doth move,
And stoop, and cringe: O then, it needs must prove
The new French tailor's motion, monthly made,
Daily to turn in Paul's, and help the trade.

1 *Monsieur* The word was often used derisively or satirically, either of actual Frenchmen or (as here) of others aping French fashions.

2 *body . . . speak French* i.e., through his dress and bearing

5 *durst* dared. The Monsieur is a coward, afraid of foreign travel and perhaps of foreign wars.

6 *half-way tree* 'Evidently a landmark on the way to Dover' (Herford & Simpsons)

9 *get* beget, conceive

10 *French disease* venereal disease *labours* suffers

12 *dam* mother

14 *stoop, and cringe* Such obsequiousness suggests that the Monsieur is a courtier. *prove* prove to be, be found (OED 8)

15 *motion* puppet, mannequin (OED 13b): punning on *motion* as moving, stooping etc. (ll.13–14) *monthly made* i.e., to suit the new fashion every month

16 *turn* 'take a turn', promenade *Paul's* 'the middle aisle of St Paul's Cathedral' (Donaldson), down which people walked to display their fashions.
help the trade i.e., The tailor is employing the man as a model to advertise his wares.

Robert Herrick

53 : Corinna's Going A-Maying

[Herrick's poetry is remarkable for its brevity, lightness and grace—and frequent superficiality. This invitation to a girl to join the May-morning festivities of spring and love is one of his more elaborate pieces. The blend of simple lyricism with classical allusions, a motif of mock-religious conceits, and finally a deeper sense of time and death, carries the *Carpe diem* convention (see p. 119) towards the intricacies of Metaphysical poetry.]

Get up, get up, for shame! The blooming morn
Upon her wings presents the god unshorn.
    See how Aurora throws her fair
    Fresh-quilted colours through the air:
    Get up, sweet slug-a-bed, and see
    The dew-bespangling herb and tree:
Each flower hath wept and bow'd toward the east
Above an hour since, yet you not drest,
    Nay, not so much as out of bed,
    When all the birds have matins said,
    And sung their thankful hymns? 'Tis sin,
    Nay, profanation, to keep in
Whenas a thousand virgins on this day
Spring sooner than the lark, to fetch in May.

Rise and put on your foliage, and be seen
To come forth, like the spring-time, fresh and green,
    And sweet as Flora: take no care
    For jewels for your gown or hair.
    Fear not: the leaves will strew
    Gems in abundance upon you.

Besides, the childhood of the day has kept,
Against you come, some orient pearls unwept:
Come, and receive them while the light
Hangs on the dew-locks of the night,
And Titan on the eastern hill
Retires himself, or else stands still
Till you come forth. Wash, dress, be brief in praying:
Few beads are best when once we go a-Maying.

Come, my Corinna, come! and coming, mark
How each field turns a street, each street a park,
Made green and trimm'd with trees! see how
Devotion gives each house a bough
Or branch! Each porch, each door, ere this,
An Ark, a Tabernacle is,
Made up of white-thorn neatly interwove,
As if here were those cooler shades of love.
Can such delights be in the street
And open fields, and we not see't?
Come, we'll abroad: and let's obey
The proclamation made for May,
And sin no more, as we have done, by staying:
But, my Corinna, come, let's go a-Maying.

There's not a budding boy or girl this day
But is got up and gone to bring in May.
A deal of youth ere this is come
Back, and with white-thorn laden, home.
Some have despatch'd their cakes and cream
Before that we have left to dream;
And some have wept and woo'd, and plighted troth,
And chose their priest, ere we can cast off sloth.
Many a green-gown has been given,
Many a kiss, both odd and even:
Many a glance, too, has been sent
From out the eye, love's firmament:
Many a jest told of the keys betraying
This night, and locks pick'd: yet we're not a-Maying.

Come, let us go, while we are in our prime,
And take the harmless folly of the time.
We shall grow old apace, and die
Before we know our liberty.
Our life is short, and our days run
As fast away as does the sun.
And as a vapour or a drop of rain
Once lost, can ne'er be found again,
So when or you or I are made
A fable, song, or fleeting shade,
All love, all liking, all delight
Lies drown'd with us in endless night.
Then while time serves, and we are but decaying,
Come, my Corinna, come: let's go a-Maying.

2 *wings* Aurora (see l.3n) usually does not fly: she rides in a chariot. Perhaps *upon her wing* = 'moving swiftly' or 'ready to start' (OED *wing* 13b) *god unshorn* Apollo the sun-god, with long golden hair

3 *Aurora* or Eos, goddess of the morning light

4 *quilted* stitched like a quilt—hence embroidered (?); or else piled up, padded

6 *dew-bespangling* sparkling with dewdrops as though with spangles (cf OED *spangling*)

7 *wept . . . east* i.e., mourned its sins and said its prayers. The 'tears' are dewdrops; flowers turn east towards the morning sun. In Europe, churches—and hence worshippers—face eastward, towards Jerusalem.

10 *matins* morning prayers

11 *thankful* offering thanks to God

11–12 *sin . . . profanation* climax of the mock-religious motif

15 *foliage* i.e., clothes, compared to a tree's new spring 'dress'

17 *Flora* goddess of flowers and the springtime *take no care* do not bother

20 *gems* i.e., flowers

21 *childhood . . . day* i.e., morning

22 *Against you come* to await your coming *orient* radiant, lustrous (like pearls brought of old from the east or orient) *pearls* i.e., dewdrops *unwept* i.e., not yet shed or spent

24 *dew-locks* 'dewy hair' or locks (L.C. Martin). The dewy foliage

really belongs to the night, though the sunlight glints (*hangs*) on it.

25 *Titan* Helios, sun-god among the Titans or older dynasty of classical gods; hence the sun.

26 *retires himself* withdraws

28 *beads* prayer-beads—but also ornamental beads, following from ll.17–18. True religion is jocularly dislodged by 'love's religion'.

30 *each field turns a street* with the crowds *each street a park* by the decorations of leaves and flowers

32 *devotion* i.e., to love

33 *ere this* i.e, before your coming

34 *Ark* the Ark of the Covenant, the chest containing the books of the Jewish law (Exodus 25:8–22) *Tabernacle* vessel in a church containing the holy bread of the Eucharist. Also a Biblical word for a tent—hence 'cooler shades' (l.36).

35, 46 *white-thorn* hawthorn or may: flowering in May and traditionally used in May-day celebrations. Cf *The Shepherd's Calendar* 'May' l.13.

39 *abroad* go out

41 *staying* delaying

45 *a deal* a large number, a band

49 *plighted troth* pledged marriage

51 *green-gown* 'gown soiled by lying on grass' (L.C. Martin): i.e., many lovers have lain down together

52 *both odd and even* both one-sided and mutual (?)

54 *firmament* the sky, with its stars: the mistress's eye spreads a similar light over love's world

55–56 *keys . . . locks pick'd* so that young men can enter their mistresses' chambers—but with an obvious sexual innuendo

57 *prime* (a) youth (b) springtime

58 *take* accept, seize *of the time* appropriate to this age or time of life

60 *know our liberty* i.e., exercise our love fully and freely

65 *or . . . or* either . . . or

66 *a fable* i.e., merely matter for a story
fleeting shade vanishing ghost or spirit

68 *endless night* translates Catullus' famous phrase *nox perpetua* (Cf. 51.8)

69 *serves* is at our service, is favourable *but decaying* only dying, not yet dead

Christopher Marlowe

54 : From *Hero and Leander*

[Marlowe left behind two sections of his unfinished *Hero and Leander*. George Chapman added four more 'sestiads' and published the full poem in 1598. Marlowe's lush yet delicate vivacity could not be matched by Chapman; but the whole still marks a high point of the Ovidian erotic-mythological tale, equalled in English only by Shakespeare's *Venus and Adonis*.

Leander of Abydos loved Hero of Sestos across the Hellespont (modern Dardanelles strait, in Turkey). Hero was a priestess of Aphrodite or Venus and hence, by a paradoxical law, herself bound to chastity. So Leander would swim secretly to her at night, till he perished in a storm. On seeing his cast-up body, Hero drowned herself. This extract describes how the two first met and fell in love.

The story was told by the Greek poet Musaeus (5th century A.D.). Marlowe knew the Latin translation by Marcus Musurus, and echoes it closely at points. Of course he also knew, and used, the imaginary letters between the lovers in Ovid's *Heroides*.]

The men of wealthy Sestos, every year,
For his sake whom their goddess held so dear,
Rose-cheek'd Adonis, kept a solemn feast.
Thither resorted many a wand'ring guest
To meet their loves; such as had none at all,
Came lovers home from this great festival.

. . . .

On this feast-day—O cursed day and hour!—
Went Hero thorow Sestos, from her tower
To Venus' temple, where unhappily,
As after chanc'd, they did each other spy.
So fair a church as this had Venus none:
The walls were of discolour'd jasper-stone,

Wherein was Proteus carv'd, and o'erhead
A lively vine of green sea-agate spread
Where by one hand light-headed Bacchus hung,
And with the other, wine from grapes out-wrung.
Of crystal shining fair the pavement was:
The town of Sestos call'd it Venus' glass.
There you might see the gods, in sundry shapes,
Committing heady riots, incest, rapes:
For know, that underneath this radiant floor
Was Danaë's statue in a brazen tower;
Jove slily stealing from his sister's bed
To dally with Idalian Ganymede,
And for his love Europa bellowing loud,
And tumbling with the rainbow in a cloud;
Blood-quaffing Mars heaving the iron net
Which limping Vulcan and his Cyclops set;
Love kindling fire, to burn such towns as Troy;
Silvanus weeping for the lovely boy
That now is turn'd into a cypress-tree,
Under whose shade the wood-gods love to be.
And in the midst a silver altar stood:
There Hero, sacrificing turtles' blood,
Vail'd to the ground, veiling her eyelids close;
And modestly they open'd as she rose.
Thence flew Love's arrow with the golden head,
And thus Leander was enamoured.
Stone-still he stood, and evermore he gaz'd,
Till with the fire that from his countenance blaz'd
Relenting Hero's gentle heart was strook:
Such force and virtue hath an amorous look.
    It lies not in our power to love or hate,
For will in us is over-rul'd by fate.
When two are stript, long ere the course begin,
We wish that one should lose, the other win;
And one especially do we affect
Of two gold ingots, like in each respect.
The reason no man knows: let it suffice,
What we behold is censur'd by our eyes.

Where both deliberate, the love is slight:
Whoever lov'd, that lov'd not at first sight?
He kneel'd; but unto her devoutly pray'd.
Chaste Hero to herself thus softly said,
'Were I the saint he worships, I would hear him.'
And, as she spake those words, came somewhat near him.
He started up: she blush'd as one asham'd,
Wherewith Leander much more was inflam'd.
He touch'd her hand; in touching it she trembled:
Love deeply grounded, hardly is dissembled.
These lovers parley'd by the touch of hands:
True love is mute, and oft amazed stands.
Thus while dumb signs their yielding hearts entangled,
The air with sparks of living fire was spangled;
And night, deep-drench'd in misty Acheron,
Heav'd up her head, and half the world upon
Breath'd darkness forth: dark night is Cupid's day.
And now begins Leander to display
Love's holy fire, with words, with sighs and tears,
Which like sweet music enter'd Hero's ears;
And yet at every word she turn'd aside,
And always cut him off as he replied.

. . . .

Which makes him quickly re-enforce his speech,
And her in humble manner thus beseech:
'Though neither gods nor men may thee deserve,
Yet for her sake whom you have vow'd to serve,
Abandon fruitless cold virginity,
The gentle queen of love's sole enemy.
Then shall you most resemble Venus' nun,
When Venus' sweet rites are perform'd and done.
Flint-breasted Pallas joys in single life;
But Pallas and your mistress are at strife.
Love, Hero, then, and be not tyrannous,
But heal the heart that thou hast wounded thus,
Nor stain thy youthful years with avarice:
Fair fools delight to be accounted nice.
The richest corn dies, if it be not reap'd:

Beauty alone is lost, too warily kept.'
These arguments he us'd, and many more,
Wherewith she yielded, that was won before.

2 *their goddess* Venus, who had a temple in Sestos

3 *Adonis* a hunter, beloved of Venus, who died while hunting a boar (see Ovid's *Metamorphoses* X.519–739). He seems to derive from an ancient vegetation god; rites like those described here, going back to early fertility rituals, were common in the ancient world. *Rose-cheek'd* so also in *Venus and Adonis* l.3. It is uncertain which is the earlier poem. *solemn* ceremonial, magnificent

4 *guest* stranger (OED 2): like Leander, from Abydos

8 *thorow* through *her tower* where she lived with the other virgins of Venus

10 *after* afterwards (referring to 'unhappily')

11 *church* i.e., temple. Such Christian terms underscore the half-serious, half-ironic equation of love and religion throughout. Cf 'saint' (l.179), 'Venus' nun' (l.319)

12 *discolour'd* multi-coloured, variegated (OED 3)

13 *Proteus* sea-god famous for his power to change form

14 *lively* lifelike *sea-agate* i.e., sea-green agate, or perhaps with wavy markings (OED *sea* 23). Natural objects like the vine are artificially rendered in stone. This vein of imagination infuses the poem with its distinctive blend of spontaneous emotion and delicate artifice.

15 *Bacchus* the god of wine, identical with Dionysus the fertility god, *light-hearted* from drinking and revelry

19–20 Suggests that sexual attraction and licence are the law of the poem's universe.

20 *heady* violent, passionate

21 *underneath . . . floor* i.e., visible through the transparent crystal

22 *Danaë* was kept locked in a tower; but Zeus (Jupiter), who loved her, visited her in the form of a shower of gold.

23 *Jove* Zeus or Jupiter *his sister* Hera or Juno, also his wife. Calling her 'his sister' suggests the 'incest' of l.144.

24 *Ganymede* a beautiful youth, carried off by Jupiter from Mount Ida (hence *Idalian*) to be his cup-bearer

25 *Europa* carried away by Zeus in the shape of a bull (hence *bellowing*)

26 Does not allude to any of Zeus' loves. Perhaps a reference to his role as Jupiter Elicius or rain-giver.

27–28 Venus, wife of Vulcan the lame god of fire, loved Mars the war-god (hence *blood-quaffing*). Vulcan captured them together in a net.

28 *Cyclops* one-eyed giants, Vulcan's assistants

29 The Trojan War began from Menelaus and Paris' dispute over Helen. Troy was finally burnt: love kindles the destructive power of Vulcan as well as of Mars.

30 *Silvanus* a wood-god. Loved Cyparissus, whom Apollo (who also loved the latter) changed to a cypress tree. *lovely* (a) beautiful (b) inspiring love

34 *turtles'* turtle-doves'. As affectionate birds pairing for life, sacred to Venus and said to draw her chariot.

35 *vail'd* bowed, bent in obeisance (OED 8, from this passage) *vailing . . . close* lowering her eyes

37 *with the golden head* i.e., causing love. Cupid's leaden arrow caused hate.

41 *strook* struck

42 *virtue* power, property

44 This tragical principle is applied to young love in playful irony —yet borne out by the ending of the story. Such blend of comic and tragic perceptions of love is common in the Elizabethan epyllion, after such models as Chaucer's *Troilus and Criseyde*. But ll.169–74 reduce this 'fate' to mere human caprice.

45 *stript* to run a race (*course*)

47 *affect* covet, prefer (OED 2)

48 *like* alike

50 *censur'd* judged, valued *eyes* i.e., not the reason or brain

53 *unto her* i.e., not to the goddess

60 *deeply grounded* solidly based, profound *hardly* with difficulty (OED 6)

62 *amazed* stupefied, confused (OED 1, 2)—hence silent

64 *sparks . . . fire* stars: it is evening. But the phrase suggests 'Love's holy fire' (l.193).

65 *Acheron* a river of the underworld, hence of darkness and death

67 *dark . . . day* i.e., Love is most active at night.

72 *replied* not 'answered', as Hero has not spoken. Perhaps 'repeats' (his interrupted speech): a rare sense (OED 7)

76 *her* i.e., Venus'

78 *gentle* either 'noble' or 'soft, mild-mannered'. Virginity is personified as Venus and Cupid's enemy.

80 *Venus' sweet rites* obviously not temple rites but the act of love

81 *Flint-breasted* stony-hearted *Pallas* Athene or Minerva, goddess of wisdom and inviolate virgin—hence 'at strife' with Venus. (See Ovid, *Metamorphoses* V. 375.)

83 *tyrannous* stock Petrarchan term for an unyielding mistress

84 Another Petrarchan convention: by yielding, the mistress can heal the 'wound' she herself has caused.

85 *avarice* greed or miserliness—in guarding her youth and beauty. The following lines illustrate the *Carpe diem* convention (see p. 119).

86 *accounted* thought, adjudged *nice* coy, reserved (OED 5)

88 *alone* i.e., without a partner

Edmund Spenser

The Faerie Queene

[*The Faerie Queene* is the most important non-dramatic poem of the Elizabethan age and, with *Paradise Lost*, of the English Renaissance. Spenser seems to have conceived of the work at least as early as 1580; even so, he left behind only a little over six books of the projected twelve. Books I to III appeared in 1590, Books IV to VI in 1596. The fragmentary Book VII (Cantos 6, 7 and part of 8) were printed in his 1609 *Works*.

Gloriana (among other things an obvious figure of Queen Elizabeth I) is queen of the land of Faerie. The Faerie race seems essentially human in kind, but their world is full of mythic and supernatural forces, as of love and adventure. This makes *The Faerie Queene* one of the greatest romantic epics of the European Renaissance. But it also carries a complex allegory harking back to the Middle Ages in its basic mode. One important line of allegory is topical and historical, but the central one is moral and spiritual: a pattern derived from Aristotle's *Nicomachean Ethics* as adopted to Christian morals and doctrine and finally transformed by Renaissance Neo-Platonism.

Spenser explains his plan in a letter to Sir Walter Ralegh. Gloriana is holding a great twelve-day feast. Each day, a supplicant appears seeking her aid in distress, and she assigns one of her knights to the task. These knights come to exemplify the basic private virtues of Christian moral life: in the six completed books respectively, Holiness, Temperance, Chastity (i.e., virtuous love), Friendship (nominally: practically a continuation of Book III), Justice and Courtesy.

The various episodes, and the characters involved in them, express a rich harmony of allegorical meaning. Running through the whole is the figure of Prince Arthur, aiding the other knights like a superior force of heroic spiritual power. He is himself in love with Gloriana, and the poem had been planned to end with their marriage. There would have followed another sequence of twelve books illustrating twelve chief public or political virtues.

The Faerie Queene was once read for its richness of description and imagery, and its lush, designedly archaic diction. Spenser was the 'poet's poet', a major influence from the early seventeenth-century 'Spenserians' to the nineteenth-century Romantics and Victorians. The modern approach concentrates, sometimes even to excess, on the rigours of the allegory and iconography. A full response will obviously integrate the two approaches. *The Faerie Queene* does not lend itself to reading in excerpts; but the one full episode and three shorter descriptive passages included here point to the wealth of this treasure house of the Renaissance poetic imagination.

See Introduction, pp. 20-21.]

55 The Wood Of Error: *The Faerie Queene* I.1.7, 10–27

[The hero of Book I is the Red-Cross Knight, so called from the arms on his shield, and thereby identified with St George, the patron saint of England. As the Knight of Holiness, he sets out to aid Una ('the One')—Truth, hence the True Church—a princess whose parents (Adam and Eve) have been beseiged in their kingdom by a dragon (Satan, who cast mankind into original sin by tempting Adam and Eve). Soon after setting out, Red-Cross, Una and their attendant dwarf shelter from a storm in the 'Wood of Error': moral and spiritual error, ultimately the Catholic doctrine that Spenser (a staunch Protestant) would regard as doctrinal error. Finally they encounter Error incarnate, half woman and half serpent. The Knight slays her.]

Enforc'd to seek some covert nigh at hand,
A shady grove not far away they spied
That promis'd aid the tempest to withstand:
Whose lofty trees, y-clad with summer's pride,
Did spread so broad, that heaven's light did hide,

Not perceble with power of any star;
And all within were paths and alleys wide
With footing worn, and leading inland far.
Fair harbour that them seems; so in they enter'd are.

[The next two stanzas chiefly describe the trees in the wood.]

Led with delight, they thus beguile the way
Until the blust'ring storm is overblown;
When, weening to return whence they did stray,
They cannot find that path which first was shown
But wander to and fro in ways unknown,
Farthest from end then, when they nearest ween,
That makes them doubt their wits be not their own:
So many paths, so many turnings seen,
That which of them to take, in diverse doubt they been.

At last, resolving forward still to fare
Till that some end they find, or in or out,
That path they take, that beaten seem'd most bare
And like to lead the labyrinth about;
Which, when by tract they hunted had throughout,
At length it brought them to a hollow cave
Amid the thickest woods. The champion stout
Eftsoons dismounted from his courser brave,
And to the dwarf a while his needless spear he gave.

'Be well aware,' quoth then that lady mild,
'Lest sudden mischief ye too rash provoke.
The danger hid, the place unknown and wild,
Breeds dreadful doubts: oft fire is without smoke,
And peril without show. Therefore your stroke,
Sir Knight, withhold, till further trial made.'
'Ah, lady,' said he, 'shame were to revoke
The forward footing for an hidden shade.
Virtue gives herself light, through darkness for to wade.'

'Yea, but,' quoth she, 'the peril of this place
I better wot than you, though now too late
To wish you back return with foul disgrace.
Yet wisdom warns, whilst foot is in the gate,
To stay the step, ere forced to retreat.
This is the wand'ring wood, this Error's den,
A monster vile, whom God and man does hate;
Therefore I rede, Beware.' 'Fly, fly,' quoth then
The fearful dwarf, 'This is no place for living men.'

But full of fire and greedy hardiment,
The youthful knight could not for ought be stay'd,
But forth unto the darksome hole he went
And looked in: his glist'ring armour made
A little glooming light, much like a shade,
By which he saw the ugly monster plain:
Half like a serpent horribly display'd,
But th'other half did woman's shape retain,
Most loathsome, filthy, foul, and full of vile disdain.

And as she lay upon the dirty ground,
Her huge long tail her den all overspread,
Yet was in knots and many boughts upwound,
Pointed with mortal sting. Of her there bred
A thousand young ones, which she daily fed,
Sucking upon her pois'nous dugs, each one
Of sundry shapes, yet all ill-favoured.
Soon as that uncouth light upon them shone,
Into her mouth they crept, and sudden all were gone.

Their dam upstart, out of her den effray'd,
And rushed forth, hurling her hideous tail
About her cursed head, whose folds display'd
Were stretch'd now forth at length without entrail.
She look'd about, and seeing one in mail
Armed to point, sought back to turn again:
For light she hated as the deadly bale,

Ay wont in desert darkness to remain,
Where plain none might her see, nor she see any plain.

Which when the valiant elf perceiv'd, he leapt
As lion fierce upon the flying prey,
And with his trenchant blade her boldly kept
From turning back, and forced her to stay.
Therewith enrag'd, she loudly 'gan to bray,
And turning fierce, her speckled tail advanc'd,
Threat'ning her angry sting, him to dismay,
Who, nought aghast, his mighty hand enhanc'd:
The stroke down from her head unto her shoulder glanc'd.

Much daunted with that dint, her sense was daz'd;
Yet kindling rage, her self she gather'd round,
And all at once her beastly body rais'd,
With double forces, high above the ground;
Tho, wrapping up her wreathed stern around,
Leapt fierce upon his shield, and her huge train
All suddenly about his body wound,
That hand or foot to stir he strove in vain:
God help the man so wrapt in Error's endless train.

His lady, sad to see his sore constraint,
Cried out, 'Now, now, Sir Knight, show what ye be!
Add faith unto your force, and be not faint:
Strangle her, else she sure will strangle thee.'
That when he heard, in great perplexity,
His gall did grate for grief and high disdain;
And knitting all his force, got one hand free,
Wherewith he gripp'd her gorge with so great pain
That soon to loose her wicked bands did her constrain.

Therewith she spew'd out of her filthy maw
A flood of poison, horrible and black,
Full of great lumps of flesh and gobbets raw,
Which stunk so vildly, that it forc'd him slack

His grasping hold, and from her turn him back.
Her vomit full of books and papers was,
With loathly frogs and toads, which eyes did lack
And creeping sought way in the weedy grass:
Her filthy parbreak all the place defiled has.

As when old Father Nilus 'gins to swell
With timely pride above the Egyptian vale,
His fatty waves do fertile slime outwell
And overflow each plain and lowly dale;
But when his later spring 'gins to avale,
Huge heaps of mud he leaves, wherein there breed
Ten thousand kinds of creatures, partly male
And partly female, of his fruitful seed:
Such ugly monstrous shapes elsewhere may no man read.

The same so sore annoyed has the knight,
That well-nigh choked with the deadly stink,
His forces fail, ne can no longer fight:
Whose courage when the fiend perceiv'd to shrink,
She poured forth, out of her hellish sink,
Her fruitful cursed spawn of serpents small,
Deformed monsters, foul, and black as ink,
Which swarming, all about his legs did crawl,
And him encumber'd sore, but could not hurt at all.

As gentle shepherd, in sweet even-tide
When ruddy Phoebus 'gins to welk in west,
High on a hill, his flock to viewen wide,
Marks which do bite their hasty supper best,
A cloud of cumbrous gnats do him molest,
All striving to infix their feeble stings,
That from their noyance he nowhere can rest,
But with his clownish hands their tender wings
He brusheth oft, and oft doth mar their murmurings:

Thus ill bestead, and fearful more of shame

Than of the certain peril he stood in,
Half furious unto his foe he came,
Resolv'd in mind all suddenly to win
Or soon to lose, before he once would lin,
And strook at her with more than manly force,
That from her body, full of filthy sin,
He raft her hateful head without remorse.
A stream of coal-black blood forth gushed from her corse.

Her scatter'd brood, soon as their parent dear
They saw so rudely falling to the ground,
Groaning full deadly, all with troublous fear
Gather'd themselves about her body round,
Weening their wonted entrance to have found
At her wide mouth; but being there withstood,
They flocked all about her bleeding wound
And sucked up their dying mother's blood,
Making her death their life, and eke her hurt their good.

That detestable sight him much amaz'd
To see th'unkindly imps, of heaven accurst,
Devour their dam: on whom while so he gaz'd,
Having all satisfied their bloody thirst,
Their bellies swoll'n he saw with fullness burst,
And bowels gushing forth: well worthy end
Of such as drunk her life, the which them nurs'd
Now needeth him no lenger labour spend:
His foes have slain themselves, with whom he should contend.

His lady, seeing all that chanc'd from far,
Approach'd in haste to greet his victory
And said, 'Fair Knight, born under happy star,
Who see your vanquish'd foes before you lie,
Well worthy be you of that armorie
Wherein you have great glory won this day,
And prov'd your strength on a strong enemy,

Your first adventure! Many such I pray,
And henceforth ever wish, that like succeed it may.'

4 *y-clad* Y- is one of many archaic affixes used in *The Faerie Queene*, as in *The Shepherd's Calendar*. *summer's pride* i.e., leaves

6 *perceable* 'piercable', penetrable *power* i.e., light *star* includes the sun

8 *footing* walking, treading

9 *harbour* shelter (pun with *arbour*) *that them seems* it seems to them

10 *beguile* pass delightfully

11 *overblown* blown over, subsided

12 *weening* thinking, wishing *whence they did stray* (to) the path they had strayed from

15 *end* their goal *ween* think

16 *doubt* fear

18 *diverse* 'turning or impelling in different directions; diverting, distracting' (OED 4)

20 'Till they reach a destination either within or outside the wood'

21 *beaten seem'd most bare* i.e., was the most trodden or used

22 *like* likely *about* around, through

23 *by tract* either 'in course of time' (OED 1) or 'through their travel or course' (OED 8)

25 *stout* strong, bold

26 *eftsoons* thereupon, immediately

27 *needless* unnecessary, superfluous. The spear was used on horseback: it could not be wielded in a thick wood.

29 *rash* rashly

31 *doubts* fears (cf. l.16)

32 *show* visible sign

33 *trial* testing, investigation *made* i.e., is made

34 *shame were* it would be shameful

34–5 *to revoke . . . shade* not to go forward for fear of an unseen evil *shade* phantom, spectre, evil spirit

36 *wade* go (OED 1)

38 *wot* know

38–9 'though it is now too late to wish that you might return, which could only be with foul disgrace'

40 *whilst . . . gate* while you are at the 'entrance' or start of a situation

41 *stay* hold back *ere forced* before (one is) forced

42 *wand'ring wood* i.e., the wood where one wanders or loses one's way. Pun on Latin *error*, literally 'to wander'.

43 *whom God and man does hate* Interesting double syntax. *Whom* implies that Error is the object, hated by God and man; but the singular *does* implies that Error hates *them*.

44 *rede* advise

45 *fearful* full of fear

46 *greedy* eager, keen (OED 3) *hardiment* boldness

47 *for ought* for anything *stay'd* restrained

48 *darksome* dark, gloomy

50 *glooming* dark; but also 'sullen, melancholy'. This line might have suggested Milton's famous phrase 'darkness visible' (*Paradise Lost* I.62).

52 *display'd* unfolded, spread out (the late Latin sense)

54 *disdain* loathsomeness: a unique passive use (OED 3b)

57 *boughts* coils, folds (pronounced 'bouts')

58 *pointed* ending in a point *mortal* deadly *bred* were, or had been, born

60–61 *each . . . shapes* May imply that *each* of the young kept changing shape; but probably just 'each one a different shape'

61 *ill-favoured* ugly

62 *uncouth* unknown, unaccustomed

63 *into her mouth they crept* as young adders allegedly did

64 *dam* mother *upstart* started up, sprang up

66 *display'd* See l.52n.

67 *entrail* coiling, entwining (OED 1b)

68 *mail* armour

69 *armed to point* fully armed

70 *bale* evil; but also a big fire (OED sb2). All light seemed such to Error.

71 *ay* always *wont* accustomed *desert* 'deserted', solitary

72 *plain* plainly

73 *elf* a supernatural being; hence one of the Faerie race (OED 4: see headnote). Red-Cross is actually human, of English or Saxon royal stock, but stolen in infancy by a Faerie. See *FQ* I.x.65.

75 *trenchant* sharp

77 *bray* cry, yell (cf. 9. 35)

78 *speckled* spotted, stained—i.e., evil. (Cf. 'speckled vanity': Milton, *Nativity Ode* l.136) *advanc'd* raised

79 *threat'ning* i.e., threatening with, brandishing

80 *nought aghast* not at all afraid *enhanc'd* lifted (OED 1)

82 *dint* stroke

83 *kindling* rousing, stirring up *her self* i.e., her form

84 *beastly body* i.e., her serpent-like lower parts. Raising these indicates a moral inversion.

86 *wreathed stern* coiled tail or posterior *around* in circles or loops(?)

87, 90 *train* tail

92 *show what ye be* show your strength, show what you are made of

93 *faith* confidence, but with obvious religious meaning for the Knight of Holiness. Hence *force* might imply the Christian moral virtue of fortitude or moral strength.

95 *perplexity* a physically entangled or confused state (OED 3); also simply 'distress' (OED 1b)

96 *gall* 'spirit to resent injury or insult' (OED 3b) *grate* offend, oppress (him)

97 *knitting* joining, gathering

98 *gorge* throat

103 *vildly* archaic variant of *vilely* *forc'd him slack* forced him to slacken

105 *books and papers* Error thus becomes intellectual, especially theological error—above all that of Catholicism, for a staunch Protestant like Spenser.

106 *eyes did lack* Error is allegorically blind

107 *weedy* covered with weeds

108 *parbreak* vomit

109 *Father Nilus* i.e., the river Nile. The clay left by the regular (*timely*, l.110), annual flooding of the Nile was thought to generate animal life spontaneously. There seems to be something grotesque about the ascription of pregnancy (*swell*, *fertile*) to 'Father' Nile.

110 *pride* splendour, magnificence *vale* valley, river-plain

111 *fatty* 'full of fertilizing matter' (OED 3) *outwell* pour out, ooze out

113 'When, later on, his flow begins to abate'

117 *read* see, discern (OED 4: peculiar to Spenser)

118 *annoyed* harmed, injured (OED 4)

122 *sink* stomach (OED 3b)

123 *fruitful* prolific, abundant

124 *ink* cf. 'books and papers', l.105
127 *gentle* mild, peaceful (by the nature of the shepherd's trade?)
128 *ruddy* red *Phoebus* Helios or Apollo, the sun-god; hence the sun *welk* fade
129 *viewen* infinitive *-en* ending. Cf. *bene,* 10.12.
130 *hasty* eaten in haste before they return to their fold
131 *cumbrous* distressing, annoying (OED 2)
133 *noyance* annoyance, irritation
134 *clownish* rustic, hence rough or rude (earlier meanings)
135 *mar* 'interrupt or stop' (OED 1)
136 *bestead* placed, circumstanced
138 *furious* mad
139 *suddenly* immediately, in this very bout
140 *lin* stop, leave
143 *raft* reft, cut off
146 *rudely* violently (OED 1)
147 *deadly* as if about to die
149 *weening* thinking *wonted* customary
150 *withstood* obstructed, prevented
153 *eke* also, further
155 *unkindly* unnatural (*kind,* nature) *imps* offspring, young; hence 'children of hell' or evil spirits
159 *bowels* entrails
161 *lenger* earlier form of *longer*
167 *armorie* i.e., coat-of-arms: the red cross of St George
171 'That similar adventures may succeed or follow it'

56 Phaedria's Island: *The Faerie Queene* II.vi. 12–17

[Among the temptations that Sir Guyon, the Knight of Temperance and hero of Book II, faces is idle, effeminate mirth as exemplified by the nymph Phaedria. She inveigles her victims on a rudderless boat to a floating island—obvious symbols of drift and laxity—set in a lake of idleness. Before accosting Guyon, Phaedria brings here one of his enemies, the knight Cymochles ('one who constantly fluctuates'), embodiment of wayward indulgence. Their arrival is followed by this account of the island.]

It was a chosen plot of fertile land,
Amongst wide waves set like a little nest
As if it had by Nature's cunning hand
Been choicely pick'd out from all the rest,
And laid forth for ensample of the best.
No dainty flower or herb that grows on ground,
No arboret with painted blossoms drest
And smelling sweet, but there it might be found
To bud out fair, and her sweet smells throw all around.

No tree whose branches did not bravely spring;
No branch whereon a fine bird did not sit;
No bird but did her shrill notes sweetly sing;
No song but did contain a lovely dit:
Trees, branches, birds and songs were framed fit
For to allure frail mind to careless ease.
Careless the man soon wox, and his weak wit
Was overcome of thing that did him please;
So pleased, did his wrathful purpose fair appease.

Thus when she had his eyes and senses fed
With false delights, and fill'd with pleasures vain,
Into a shady dale she oft him led
And laid him down upon a grassy plain;
And her sweet self, without dread or disdain,
She set beside, laying his head disarm'd
In her loose lap, it softly to sustain:
Where soon he slumber'd, fearing not be harm'd,
The whiles with a loud lay she thus him sweetly charm'd.

'Behold, O man, that toilsome pains dost take:
The flowers, the fields, and all that pleasant grows,
How they themselves do thine ensample make
Whiles, nothing envious, Nature them forth throws
Out of her fruitful lap; how no man knows,
They spring, they bud, they blossom fresh and fair
And deck the world with their rich pompous shows:

Yet no man for them taketh pains or care,
Yet no man to them can his careful pains compare.

The lily, lady of the flowering field,
The flower-de-luce her lovely paramour,
Bid thee to them thy fruitless labours yield
And soon leave off this toilsome weary stour.
Lo, lo, how brave she decks her bounteous bower
With silken curtains and gold coverlets,
Therein to shroud her sumptuous belamour,
Yet neither spins nor cards, ne cares nor frets,
But to her mother Nature all her care she lets.

Why then dost thou, O man, that of them all
Art lord, and eke of Nature sovereign,
Wilfully make thyself a wretched thrall
And waste thy joyous hours in needless pain,
Seeking for danger and adventures vain?
What boots it, all to have and nothing use?
Who shall him rue, that swimming in the main
Will die for thirst, and water doth refuse?
Refuse such fruitless toil, and present pleasures choose.

1 *chosen* choice, select: see l.4 below
5 *ensample of the best* an example or model of an ideal island
6 *dainty* pretty
7 *arboret* small tree or shrub *painted* i.e., colourful. A standard poetic epithet, but suggests artificiality and deceit ('false delights', l.20) *drest* decked, adorned
10 *bravely* gaily, splendidly (OED 2)
10–13 *tree . . . branch . . . bird . . . sing/song* Such interlinking of sentences was known as *concatenatio* (Latin *catena,* chain)
12 *shrill* used with no pejorative sense
13 *dit* ditty. Usually applied to the words of a song: these may be enchanted birds singing in human fashion.
14 *framed* made; but again suggests contrivance and deceit
15 *frail* i.e., morally feeble, self-indulgent
16 *wox* waxed, grew *wit* not only intelligence but the faculties generally

17 *of thing* by the thing
18 i.e., Knights were disarmed of their martial spirit.
24 *disarm'd* i.e., with helmet off
25 *sustain* support
26 *not be harm'd* not to be harmed
27 *loud* a surprising word here. Perhaps *lowed,* 'hushed, soft'
28–54 Ironically, this plea for immoral self-indulgence perverts Christ's famous words, 'Behold the fowls of the air' etc (Matthew 7:26–30)
30 *thine ensample make* provide an example for you
31 *envious* malicious, hence harmful
Nature see headnote to no.58.
34 *pompous* splendid, magnificent: no pejorative sense
36 *careful pains* i.e., the beauty produced by his careworn labour
37 *lady* mistress, woman ruler
38 *flower-de-luce* fleur-de-lis or iris (*not* the lily: cf.l.37)
39 *yield* surrender in defeat, admit as inferior
40 *soon* at once: an early sense *stour* battle, struggle: hence toil, stress (OED 3: first so used by Spenser)
41 *brave* (a) beautiful (b) proud, bold
42 *curtains . . . coverlets* i.e., the leaves and petals
43 *shroud* clothe, adorn (OED 1, 2)—but with sinister connotations of a dead man's shroud *sumptuous* splendid, handsome *belamour* beloved (French *bel amour,* fair love)
44 *cards* combs or prepares wool for spinning *ne* nor
45 *lets* leaves
47 *eke* also
48 *wilfully* willingly, deliberately (OED 1, 2); but also perversely, obstinately *thrall* captive, slave (opposed to *sovereign,* l.48)
51 *what boots it* what use or profit is it
have, and nothing use i.e., possess with enjoying
52 *rue* pity *main* the open sea

57 Mutability: *The Faerie Queene* VII.vi.1–6

[This passage, like the next, shows Spenser's combination of philosophic and myth-making power. It describes the origin and nature of Mutability (Change), conceived as a Titaness but embodying the philosophic concept of change and transience, in a remarkable Renaissance blend of classical myth and medieval allegory. It opens the 'Mutability Cantos' that constitute the fragmentary Book VII of *The Faerie Queene*.]

What man that sees the ever-whirling wheel
Of change, the which all mortal things doth sway,
But that thereby doth find and plainly feel
How Mutability in them doth play
Her cruel sports, to many men's decay?
Which that to all may better yet appear,
I will rehearse that whilom I heard say,
How she at first herself began to rear
'Gainst all the gods, and th'empire sought from them to bear.

But first, here falleth fittest to unfold
Her antique race and linage ancient,
As I have found it register'd of old
In Faerie Land 'mongst records permanent.
She was, to weet, a daughter by descent
Of those old Titans, that did whilom strive
With Saturn's son for heaven's regiment:
Whom though high Jove of kingdom did deprive,
Yet many of their stem long after did survive.

And many of them afterwards obtain'd
Great power of Jove, and high authority:
As Hecate, in whose almighty hand
He plac'd all rule and principality,
To be by her disposed diversely
To gods and men, as she them list divide;
And drad Bellona, that doth sound on high
Wars and alarums unto nations wide,
That makes both heaven and earth to tremble at her pride.

So likewise did this Titaness aspire

Rule and dominion to herself to gain,
That as a goddess men might her admire
And heavenly honours yield, as to them twain.
At first, on earth she sought it to obtain,
Where she such proof and sad examples show'd
Of her great power, to many one's great pain,
That not men only (whom she soon subdued),
But eke all other creatures her bad doings rued.

For she the face of earthly things so chang'd
That all which Nature had establish'd first
In good estate, and in meet order rang'd,
She did pervert, and all their statutes burst;
And all the world's fair frame (which none yet durst
Of gods or men to alter or misguide)
She alter'd quite, and made them all accurst
That God had blest and did, at first, provide
In that still happy state for ever to abide.

Ne she the laws of Nature only brake
But eke of justice and of policy,
And wrong of right, and bad of good did make,
And death for life exchanged foolishly:
Since which, all living wights have learnt to die
And all this world is woxen daily worse.
O piteous work of Mutability!
By which we all are subject to that curse,
And death instead of life have sucked from our Nurse.

2 *sway* rule
3 *But that . . . find* i.e., Who does not thereby find
5 *decay* ruin, destruction (OED 1b)
7 *that whilom* that (which) once
8 *rear* raise, arouse
9 *empire* rule, sway *from them* instead of them, taking away from them *bear* 'To wield (power, sway, etc.)' (OED 8)
10 *here falleth fittest* i.e, this is the fittest place (*falleth*, befalls or comes about)

11 *linage* lineage, ancestry

13 *permanent* here obviously 'old, long-standing'

14 *to weet* an empty poetic phrase: roughly 'it is to be known', 'for information'

15 *Titans* the generation of Greek gods who ruled before that of Zeus (Saturn's son: l.16): often conceived as giants. Also the descendants of the Titans proper—Hecate etc. (ll.21 ff.)—to whom Mutability is assimilated here. *whilom* see l.7

16 *regiment* rule

17 *whom* i.e, the Titans *high* lofty, great *Jove* Zeus or Jupiter

18 *stem* stock, lineage

20 *of* from

21 *Hecate* commonly the goddess of night and the moon. Here ascribed with universal powers and the special favour of Zeus, following Hesiod (*Theogony* 411–52).

22 *principality* sovereignty, princely power (OED 2)

24 *list* wished, chose

25 *drad* fearsome (variant of *dread*) *Bellona* goddess of war. Not a Titaness by any classical authority.

26 *alarums* alarms, call to war *wide* wide-ranging, far-flung

30 *admire* 'wonder or marvel at' (OED 2)

31 *them twain* those two: i.e., Hecate and Bellona

33 *sad* 'distressing, calamitous, lamentable' (OED 5f)

36 *eke* also *rued* sorrowed for, deplored

39 *meet* fit, proper *rang'd* ordered

40 *statutes* i.e., laws of their being

41 *frame* order, composition

42 *misguide* divert

43–4 *accurs't . . . blest* In Christian belief, man fell by disobeying God, and suffered the action of time and decay as a punishment. Spenser here makes Mutability the cause of man's fall.

44 *provide* prepare, arrange

45 *still* always: a common old meaning

46 *Ne* nor

47 *policy* administration, government

50 *wights* creatures, beings

51 *woxen* waxed, grown

54 *suck'd from our nurse* Even a newborn infant is tainted by original sin. But the capital N might imply that *our Nurse* = Nature.

58 Nature: *The Faerie Queene* VII.vii.5–13, 57–59

[The creative force of life was commonly mythicized as a kind of goddess, a universal generative agent or mother. 'Dame Nature' occurs in Spenser's famous 'Garden of Adonis' passage (*FQ* III.vi. 30.2). As the notes show, she is also close to Venus, goddess not only of love but of universal life, as described in the 'Temple of Venus' passage (*FQ* IV.x.44–47). Here Nature, the genetrix of continuing life in the midst of change, comes forth to judge Mutability's claim to supreme power among the gods.]

Then forth issued (great goddess) great Dame Nature,
With goodly port and gracious majesty,
Being far greater and more tall of stature
Than any of the gods or powers on high.
Yet certes, by her face and phys'nomy,
Whether she man or woman inly were,
That could not any creature well descry:
For, with a veil that wimpled every where,
Her head and face was hid, that mote to none appear.

That, some do say, was so by skill devis'd
To hide the terror of her uncouth hue,
From mortal eyes that should be sore agris'd:
For that her face did like a lion show,
That eye of wight could not endure to view.
But others tell that it so beauteous was,
And round about such beams of splendour threw,
That it the sun a thousand times did pass,
Ne could be seen, but like an image in a glass.

That well may seemen true: for well I ween
That this same day, when she on Arlo sat,
Her garment was so bright and wondrous sheen,
That my frail wit cannot devise to what
It to compare, nor find like stuff to that
As those three sacred saints, though else most wise,

Yet on Mount Tabor quite their wits forgat
When they their glorious Lord in strange disguise
Tranfigur'd saw: his garments so did daze their eyes.

In a fair plain, upon an equal hill,
She placed was in a pavilion:
Not such as craftsmen by their idle skill
Are wont for princes' states to fashion,
But th'earth herself, of her own motion,
Out of her fruitful bosom made to grow
Most dainty trees; that, shooting up anon,
Did seem to bow their bloss'ming heads full low
For homage unto her, and like a throne did show.

So hard it is for any living wight
All her array and vestiments to tell,
That old Dan Geoffrey (in whose gentle spright
The pure well-head of poesy did dwell)
In his 'Fowl's Parley' durst not with it mel,
But it transferr'd to Alan, who he thought
Had in his 'Plaint of Kind' describ'd it well:
Which who will read set forth so as it ought,
Go seek he out that Alan where he may be sought.

And all the earth far underneath her feet
Was dight with flowers, that voluntary grew
Out of the ground, and sent forth odours sweet;
Ten thousand mores of sundry scent and hue
That might delight the smell or please the view,
The which the nymphs from all the brooks thereby
Had gather'd, which they at her footstool threw,
That richer seem'd than any tapestry
That princes' bowers adorn with painted imag'ry.

And Mole himself, to honour her the more,
Did deck himself in freshest fair attire,
And his high head, that seemeth always hoar

With harden'd frosts of former winter's ire,
He with an oaken garland now did tire,
As if the love of some new nymph late seen
Had in him kindled youthful fresh desire
And made him change his gray attire to green.
Ah, gentle Mole! such joyance hath thee well beseen.

Was never so great joyance since the day
That all the gods whilom assembled were
On Haemus hill in their divine array
To celebrate the solemn bridal cheer
'Twixt Peleus and Dame Thetis pointed there,
Where Phoebus' self, that god of poets hight,
They say did sing the spousal hymn full clear,
That all the gods were ravish'd with delight
Of his celestial song, and music's wondrous might.

This great-grandmother of all creatures bred,
Great Nature, ever young yet full of eld,
Still moving, yet unmoved from her stead,
Unseen of any, yet of all beheld,
Thus sitting in her throne as I have tell'd,
Before her came Dame Mutability:
And being low before her presence fell'd,
With meek obeisance and humility
Thus 'gan her plaintive plea with words to amplify.

[After Mutability and Jove have presented their arguments, Nature delivers judgment.]

So having ended, silence long ensued;
Ne Nature to or fro spake for a space,
But with firm eyes affixt, the ground still view'd.
Meanwhile all creatures, looking in her face,
Expecting th'end of this so doubtful case,
Did hang in long suspense what would ensue,
To whether side should fall the sov'reign place.

At length she, looking up with cheerful view,
The silence brake, and gave her doom in speeches few.

'I well consider all that ye have said,
And find that all things steadfastness do hate
And changed be; yet being rightly weigh'd,
They are not changed from their first estate,
But by their change their being do dilate;
And turning to themselves at length again,
Do work their own perfection so by fate.
Then over them Change doth not rule and reign,
But they reign over Change, and do their states maintain.

Cease therefore, daughter, further to aspire,
And thee content thus to be rul'd by me:
For thy decay thou seek'st by thy desire,
But time shall come that all shall changed be,
And from thenceforth, none no more change shall see.'
So was the Titaness put down and whisht,
And Jove confirm'd in his imperial see.
Then was that whole assembly quite dismiss'd,
And Nature's self did vanish, whither no man wist.

1 *great goddess* addressed to Calliope the epic muse. In *FQ* VII.vii.1.1., Spenser had repeated his earlier invocations to Calliope (I Proem 2, VII.vi.37.9), given the awesome theme he is now treating of.

2 *port* carriage, bearing

5 *phys'nomy* physiognomy: commonly 'face', but here no doubt 'general appearance' (OED 4)

6–7 Cf. *FQ* IV.x.41.6–9, where Venus is said to be hermaphroditic or bisexual: a not uncommon attribute of the goddess of universal life. Venus and Nature are analogous figures in Spenser: see J. Nohrnberg, *The Analogy of The Faerie Queene* (1976), pp. 647–51.

6 *inly* inside, within her veil (1.8)

8 *wimpled* fell in folds (OED 4)

9 *mote* may, must

10 *That* i.e., the veil

11 *uncouth* unknown, strange *hue* form, appearance: the original sense

12 *agris'd* terrified

13 *lion* Indicates the harsh or destructive aspect of nature, balancing her creative power and fostering care. The precise iconography is hard to explain. The lion was one of the figures in Nature's crown in Alan of Lille's *The Complaint of Nature* (see l.42n.). Lions drew the chariot of Cybele, the earth-goddess whom Spenser seems to associate with Nature. The *Hieroglyphica* (4th century A.D.) of the legendary 'Horapollo' (I.20, 21) associates the lion with fearsomeness, radiance and fecundity, as here. But actually to endow Nature with a lion's face might have been Spenser's own idea.

14 'such that no living creature's eye could bear the sight'

17 *pass* surpass

18 *glass* mirror (The actual beam was too dazzling to view.)

19 *seemen* old infinitive of *seem* *ween* think, believe, imagine

20 *Arlo* a hill in Ireland, appointed as the place of trial

21 *sheen* shining

23 *like stuff to that* material like that

24 *sacred saints* Peter, James and John, before whom Christ (*their Lord*, l.26) appeared transfigured and radiant (*glorious*, l.26). See Matthew 17:1–9, Mark 9:2–9, Luke 9:28–36.

25 *Tabor* or Jebel-et-Tur, a mountain in Palestine where the Transfiguration was commonly though perhaps wrongly held to have occurred *forgat* forgot

26 *disguise* new guise or appearance (?: cf. OED 1)

27 *daze* dazzle

29 *pavilion* tent

30–36 This allies Nature's tent with the Garden of Adonis (III.vi) and Temple of Venus (IV.x), Spenser's two great allegorical set pieces on the force of universal life, and contrasts it with Phaedria's island (see above, no. **56**) and Acrasia's Bower of Bliss (II. xii), artificial seats of sinful indulgence and lust. On this nature/artifice contrast, see C.S. Lewis, *The Allegory of Love* (1936), pp. 324–8.

30 *idle* trivial, vain (OED 2)

31 *wont* accustomed *state(s)* 'costly and imposing display' (OED 17)

31, 32 *fashion, motion* pronounced 'fash-i-on', 'mot-i-on', as words ending in *-ion* commonly were in Elizabethan verse

32 *motion* impulse, volition (OED 9)

34 *dainty* beautiful, delectable *anon* at once (OED 4)

38 *vestiments* vestments, robes

39 *Dan* a title of respect like 'Master' or 'Sir'
Geoffrey Geoffrey Chaucer: see l.41n. *spright* spirit

40 *well-head* spring, fountain, origin

41 *'Fowls' Parley* In *The Parliament of Fowls* 316–18, Chaucer desists from describing Nature, referring instead to Alanus (see l.42n.). *mel* meddle

42 *it* i.e., the task of describing Nature *Alan* Alan of Lille (d. 1203): his Latin 'Complaint of Nature' has a long description of Nature.

43 *kind* Nature. (*Kindes* in the original, inexplicably. Perhaps a possessive: 'The Complaint of Nature's')

44 *which* i.e., the description of Nature *so as it ought* as it should be

45 *where he may be sought* where he (i.e., his book) is to be found

47 *dight* decked, adorned
voluntary used as adverb

49 *more(s)* a tree-stump or root; here, a plant (OED 1b, citing this line alone)

51 *thereby* beside, near (OED 2)

54 *painted imag'ry* Tapestries are actually woven, painted cloth being a cheaper substitute. Perhaps *painted* = colourful (OED 3). On the nature/artifice contrast see ll.30–36n.

55 *Mole* a river springing from Arlo Hill

57 *head* spring, source

58 *former winter's ire* the wrath or rigour of the last winter

59 *tire* attire, adorn—specifically, the head (OED 2c) with a *tire* or head-dress

63 *joyance* festivity, merriment *beseen* apparently *beseem(ed)* 'suit, fit' crossed with *seen* 65 *whilom* once

66 *Haemus* a mountain range in South-East Europe. The marriage of Peleus and Thetis actually took place on Mount Pelion.

67 *the bridal cheer* marriage festivities

68 Peleus, king of the Myrmidons, married the sea-nymph Thetis; their son was Achilles. The gods attended the wedding and gave rich gifts.

See *Iliad* 16:143, 18:84. *Dame* lady: used loosely as a female title. Cf. l.78. *pointed* appointed, arranged

69 *Phoebus* Apollo *hight* is called

74 *eld* age

75 *stead* assigned place, seat (OED 5)

79 *fell'd* fallen (in supplication)

81 *plaintive* *plaintif* in the original. Till the 18th century, *plaintive* doubled with *plaintiff*, the complainant in a lawsuit—as here. *amplify* develop, expand: a rhetorical term

83 *Ne* nor *to or fro* in favour of either side

84 *still* always, continuously

87 *suspense what* i.e., suspense as to what

88 *whether* which of the two *sovereign place* i.e., rule over the universe

89 *cheerful view* joyful appearance

90 *doom* judgment *speeches* phrases, utterances (cf. OED 9c)

93 *weigh'd* judged

94 *estate* state, condition

95 *dilate* extend, prolong, continue

96 *themselves* i.e., their original states

102 *decay* Cf. 55.5. *desire* i.e., ambition

103 *time shall come* Alluding to Doomsday, when the earth will be destroyed and all men will assume their existence in eternity. The discourse suddenly acquires a Christian tone, which reaches its height in the next, fragmentary canto of two stanzas.

105 *whisht* hushed, silent

106 *see* seat, throne 108 *wist* know

Sir John Davies

59 : From *Orchestra*

[Sir John Davies's *Orchestra* (1596) is a poem in praise of dancing in terms of the 'dance', order or harmony in the universe and in human life, guided by the cosmic power of 'Love'. The didactic content is gracefully contained in a fable of how Antinous, paying court to Ulysses' wife Penelope during her husband's absence at war, tries to induce her to dance.

The poem is in the seven-line stanza called 'rime royal', after its use by James I of Scotland in *The King's Quire* (1423–4); or, after a greater practitioner, the Chaucerian stanza.]

Dancing, bright lady, then began to be
When the first seeds whereof the world did spring,
The fire, air, earth and water, did agree
By Love's persuasion, nature's mighty king,
To leave their first disorder'd combating
    And in a dance such measure to observe,
    As all the world their motion should preserve.

Since when, they still are carried in a round
And, changing, come one in another's place;
Yet do they neither mingle nor confound,
But every one doth keep the bounded space
Wherein the dance doth bid it turn or trace.
    This wondrous miracle did Love devise,
    For dancing is Love's proper exercise.

Like this he fram'd the gods' eternal bower,
And of a shapeless and confused mass,
By his through-piercing and digesting power,
The turning vault of heaven formed was,

Whose starry wheels he hath so made to pass
As that their movings do a music frame,
And they themselves still dance unto the same.

Or if this All which round about we see,
As idle Morpheus some sick brains hath taught,
Of undivided motes compacted be,
How was this goodly architecture wrought?
Or by what means were they together brought?
They err that say they did concur by chance:
Love made them meet in a well-order'd dance.

As when Amphion with his charming lyre
Begot so sweet a siren of the air,
That with her rhetoric made the stones conspire
The ruins of a city to repair,
A work of wit and reason's wise affair,
So Love's smooth tongue, the motes such measure taught
That they join'd hands, and so the world was wrought.

How justly then is dancing termed new,
Which with the world in point of time began?
Yea, Time itself, whose birth Jove never knew
And which is far more ancient than the sun,
Had not one moment of his age outrun
When out leapt Dancing from the heap of things,
And lightly rode upon his nimble wings.

2 *first seeds* i.e., the four elements (l.3): said to have been in conflict till reconciled by Love (see below).

4 *Love* Conceived as the attracting, ordering and harmonizing force of the whole universe. The idea goes back to early Greek thought, and is reflected in Plato (*Symposium* 186–8). For the Middle Ages and Renaissance, the seminal passage was Boethius, *Consolations of Philosophy* Bk. II poem 8 (closely

followed by Chaucer in *Troilus and Criseyde* III. 1744–71). See also Spenser, 'An Hymn in Honour of Love' ll.78–98.

6 *measure* rhythm, order

7 *preserve* observe, maintain

8 *still* always *round* a circular dance

9 *changing* exchanging places as in a dance

10 *mingle* merge
confound confuse their places

12 *trace* step or tread, as in a dance *turn* also applies to a dance movement

14 *exercise* working, manifestation

15–21 The universe according to the ancient Ptolemaic model: infinite celestial space or the Empyrean (*the gods' eternal bower*) enclosing a series of revolving (*turning*) crystalline spheres in which the stars and planets are set (hence *starry wheels*).

16 *shapeless . . . mass* chaos, the unformed stuff of the universe

17 *through-piercing* penetrating, infusing *digesting* ordering, reducing to a system (OED *digest* 2)

19 *pass* move

22 *Or* now (introductory particle, like 'Now then': perhaps from Fr. *or*) (OED *or* adv.2, cited from Middle English only)
this All i.e., this total order

23 *Morpheus* god of sleep, hence of dreams or illusions

24 *undivided motes* atoms, which cannot be further divided. The Greek philosopher Epicurus taught that the universe was composed of the random union of such atoms. This 'godless' view was rejected by Christians (See l.27).
compacted composed

25 *architecture* structure, order

27 *concur* converge, unite

29–32 *Amphion* After he and his brother had captured and destroyed the city of Thebes, he rebuilt its walls by the music of his lyre
charming spell-binding, magical

30 *siren of the air* i.e., music. The sirens lured sailors to their doom by their sweet song (*Odyssey* XII. 158–200).

31 *rhetoric* 'speech', i.e., music
conspire in a good sense: agree, conjoin

33 Refers to the city: first built by wisdom (*wit*) and planning (*reason*), but rebuilt miraculously by music. *affair* action, performance (OED 5)

34 *smooth tongue* i.e., her song or 'rhetoric': no pejorative sense

35 *wrought* made

36–7 'How then can dancing be properly called "new"? It is as old as the world itself.'

38 *Jove* Jupiter. Chronos ('Time') belongs to an older generation of gods, and is identified with Jupiter's father Saturn.

41 *heap of things* i.e., chaos (see l.16n.)

42 *rode* 'moved' generally: here, flew

Michael Drayton

60 From *The Muses' Elysium*: Nymphal X

[The reign of Elizabeth I is often viewed too simply as a time of national and cultural upsurge, a golden age. It was in many ways a hard and violent age: moved by the religious and political troubles of contemporary Europe, subject also to the Queen's own authoritarian rule. Yet Elizabeth held the state together by a package of masterly strategies and compromises, assuming by the end an almost mystic authority. When religious and economic issues began to divide the nation under her inept successors, there developed a veritable cult of Elizabethan nostalgia: James I's rule, and later Charles I's, were exposed to savage contrast. Hence the cultural achievement of Elizabeth's reign acquired the status of an enduring myth of practical or political thrust, though expressed chiefly in aesthetic terms. That is why the term 'Elizabethan' still means something special today.

Late in life (published 1630), Drayton transformed pastoral convention into the compelling fantasy of a 'Muses' Elysium' or Paradise of poetry, where a troop of bright 'nymphs' and 'swains' love, sing and worship Apollo and the Muses in a landscape of perpetual spring. Designedly unreal and even escapist, Drayton's dream nonetheless had a strong social and topical relevance. As the name 'Elizium' (so spelt) punningly suggests, his paradise evokes the ideal order of Elizabeth's reign. It is contrasted with Felicia (meaning, ironically, 'the happy land'), which stands for England in James and Charles's reigns.

In the last poem of the series, a Satyr has strayed from Felicia to Elysium. The *Satyr*, a grotesque and usually savage wood-god, half man and half goat, was often made the image of *satire*, by a common etymological confusion. But Drayton's Satyr is gentle, indeed weary and pitiable, perhaps a *persona* of Drayton himself. Elysium seems to image a patron's estate in Dorset where the old poet found a retreat. The poem contains bitter satire of the times; but the overall purpose is a search for peace and rest in the idealized memories of a vanished cultural order.

In this passage, the Satyr replies to the Elysians' queries about his arrival.]

Satyr O never ask how I came to this place:
What cannot strong necessity find out?
Rather bemoan my miserable case,
Constrain'd to wander the wide world about.
With wild Sylvanus and his woody crew
In forests, I, at liberty and free,
Liv'd in such pleasures as the world ne'er knew,
Nor any rightly can conceive but we.
This jocond life we many a day enjoy'd,
Till this last age those beastly men forth brought
That all those great and goodly woods destroy'd
Whose growth their grandsires with such sufferance sought:
That fair Felicia, which was but of late
Earth's Paradise, that never had her peer,
Stands now in that most lamentable state
That not a sylvan will inhabit there,
Where in the soft and most delicious shade
In heat of summer we were wont to play,
When the long day too short for us we made,
The sliding hours so slily stole away.
By Cynthia's light, and on the pleasant lawn,
The wanton fairy we were wont to chase,
Which to the nimble cloven-footed faun
Upon the plain durst boldly bid the base.
The sportive nymphs with shouts and laughter shook
The hills and valleys in their wanton play,
Waking the echoes, their last words that took
Till at the last, they louder were than they.
The lofty high wood and the lower spring,
Sheltering the deer in many a sudden shower,

Where quires of birds oft wonted were to sing,
The flaming furnace wholly doth devour:
Once fair Felicia, but now quite defac'd,
Those braveries gone wherein she did abound,
With dainty groves, when she was highly grac'd
With goodly oak, ash, elm and beeches crown'd!
But that from heaven their judgment blinded is,
In human reason it could never be
But that they might have clearly seen by this
Those plagues their next posterity shall see.
The little infant on the mother's lap
For want of fire shall be so sore distress'd
That whilst it draws the lank and empty pap,
The tender lips shall freeze unto the breast.
The quaking cattle, which their wormstall want,
And with bleak winter's northern wind oppress'd,
Their browse and stover waxing lean and scant,
The hungry crows shall with their carrion feast.
Men wanting timber wherewith they should build,
And not a forest in Felicia found,
Shall be enforc'd upon the open field
To dig them caves for houses in the ground.
The land, thus robb'd of all her rich attire,
Naked and bare herself to heaven doth show,
Begging from thence that Jove would dart his fire
Upon those wretches that disrob'd her so.
This beastly brood by no means may abide
The name of their brave ancestors to hear,
By whom their sordid slavery is descried,
So unlike them as though not theirs they were.
Nor yet they sense nor understanding have
Of those brave muses that their country sung,
But with false lips ignobly do deprave
The right and honour that to them belong.
This cruel kind thus viper-like devour

That fruitful soil which them too fully fed:
The earth doth curse the age, and every hour
Again, that it these vip'rous monsters bred.
I, seeing the plagues that shortly are to come
Upon this people, clearly them forsook,
And thus am light into Elysium,
To whose strait search I wholly me betook.

Naiis Poor silly creature, come along with us:
Thou shalt be free of the Elysian fields.
Be not dismay'd or inly grieved thus:
This place content in all abundance yields.
We to the cheerful presence will thee bring
Of Jove's dear daughters, where in shades they sit,
Where thou shalt hear those sacred sisters sing
Most heavenly hymns, the strength and life of wit.

Claia Where to the Delphian God, upon their lyres
His priests seem ravish'd in his height of praise,
While he is crowning his harmonious quires
With circling garlands of immortal bays.

2 i.e., Pressing need led me to find the way here.
3 *case* situation
5 *Sylvanus* a classical wood-god (Latin *silva*, forest)
woody living in *woods* *crew* band (of wood-gods)
10 *beastly men* ironic from a satyr's lips: the new men look fully human but are beastly in nature.
11 *woods destroy'd* Drayton's age, like the previous one, saw much deforestation, which Drayton often laments in *Poly-Olbion* and elsewhere, seeing it as a sign of the time's decay.
12 *sufferance* pains, trouble
13 *that* so that *Felicia* England: once blessed (Latin *felix*, happy) but now degenerate. *Elysium* is more specifically Elizabethan England, as well as the realm of the poetic imagination. See headnote.
17 *delicious* pleasant, delightful
20 *sliding* slipping, fleeting

21 *Cynthia* Diana the virgin moon-goddess, hence the moon: commonly applied to Elizabeth the virgin queen
pleasant pleasing, beautiful *lawn* 'An open space between woods; a glade' (OED 1)

22, 26 *wanton* playful; but also flirtatious or even lustful

22 *wont to* accustomed to *chase* i.e., pursue in love

23 *which* i.e., the fairy *faun* another satyr-like wood-god

24 *bid the base* challenge (from the old game of 'prisoner's base'). The fairies flirtatiously led on the fauns, who were conventionally regarded as lustful.

29 *spring* young copse (cf. 10.53)

31 *wonted were* Cf. 1.22.

32 *flaming furnace* Forests were often cut down to provide wood for smelting iron.

33 *defac'd* disfigured; but also in the 16th century 'discredited, defamed'

34 *braveries* beauties, ornaments

35 *dainty* pleasant, delightful

37 'Were it not that Fate has blinded their judgment'

40 *plagues* afflictions, torments *next posterity* the next generation

43 *draws* sucks at

45 *quaking* i.e., shivering with cold *wormstall* 'An outdoor shelter for cattle in warm weather' (OED), but here obviously any cattle shed. *want* lack. There is no wood to build such sheds.

47 *browse* fodder of young shoots and twigs. *stover* 'winter food for cattle' (OED 2). With deforestation, cattle lack food in both summer and winter. *waxing* growing

49 *wanting* Cf. 1.45.

50 *And not* old construction: 'seeing that there is not', 'there not being'

55 *Jove['s] fire* the thunder

59 *descried* decried, denounced

62 *their country sung* sang of their country

63 *deprave* debase, impair

65 *viper-like* The viper is proverbially ungrateful.

70 *clearly* straight, 'cleanly' (cf. OED *clear* B5b)

71 *light* alighted, descended (from Parnassus, the hill sacred to poetry, said to overlook Elysium)

72 *strait* rigorous, diligent. Perhaps also 'narrow': the narrow pass leading to Elysium would be hard to find.
me betook applied myself

73, 81 *Naiis, Claia* Two Elysian 'Nymphs'

73 *silly* 'deserving of pity, compassion or sympathy' (OED 1)

74 *be free of* have the liberty of, be free to move about in

78, 79 *Jove's dear daughters . . . sacred Sisters* the Muses (*Jove* Jupiter)

80 *strength . . . wit* presumably said of the Muses *wit* wisdom, faculties. Here no doubt the poetic faculty in particular.

81 *the Delphian God* Apollo, whose chief temple was at Delphi

82 *in his height of praise* i.e., singing his highest praises

83 *harmonious quires* Presumably the poets encircling or following him

84 *circling* i.e., encircling the head *bays* the laurel, with which poets were crowned: *immortal* as being evergreen, but also as conferring immortal fame.

Index